Freedom from Generational Sin

Generational and Family Blessings

Freedom from Generational Sin

Generational and Family Blessings

Combined edition

Ruth Hawkey

New Wine Press

New Wine Press
An imprint of Roperpenberthy Publishing Ltd
Springfield House
23 Oatlands Drive
Weybridge KT13 9LX
United Kingdom

ISBN: 978 1 905991 89 1

Typeset by CRB Associates, Potterhanworth, Lincolnshire
Printed in the United Kingdom

Freedom from
Generational Sin

Contents

Preface

Having taught into the subject of "Generational Sin" for a number of years now, at various seminars around the country, I have found that it has often been received either with great delight or with the very relevant query, "Is this scriptural?" I hope to show that it is both scriptural and very applicable to today's Christians. My desire is that the reader will begin to see answers to some of the questions which may have puzzled them for years.

Such questions for instance as, "Why is it that I seem to be repeating the pattern of fears and phobias that obsessed my mother's life even though I have tried repeatedly to change?" Or "Why do I find pornography books so difficult to lay down?" or "What is the reason that I find the pornographic material on the Internet so difficult to resist? I have tried to withstand looking at it, I have fasted and prayed, I have cried out to God, but all to little or no effect. I am still hooked."

Or the questioner may ask, "Why am I so fascinated with the occult? My family are second generation Christians, so where does the strong interest spring from?" Or as one person said to me, "My grandfather was an abuser, my father was an abuser, I have been an abuser. What can I do to stop my children from falling into the same trap?"

I hope to show that, whilst such folk have the responsibility of dealing with their own personal sin, nevertheless many of them may also be battling against the sins of their ancestors. It may be that they are inheriting the weaknesses of previous generations, and until those weaknesses are recognised, confessed and repented of, they will continue to struggle to walk into the freedom which Christ died to bring them.

This book is a response to those people who have heard the teaching on "Generational Sin", and who have asked that the teaching be presented in written form for their future reference and help. My hope and prayer is that it will be a blessing to most people and a means of release to many in the Body of Christ.

Ruth Hawkey

Chapter 1
The Laws of God

Whoever we are, and wherever we have been born, whether it is in Britain, Jamaica, New Zealand or as far away as in the deepest forests of North Borneo, it is an undoubted truth that we are all born into a family. This lineage will have a certain amount of generational blessing as well as generational sin built into it. For none of us have come into this world born to completely innocent parents with an impeccable pedigree, and whilst it is true that some of us have inherited more good than evil, all of us to some extent, have to carry our generational baggage around with us!

Most of us carry a crate-load of mixed blessings and cursing, for it is a truism that in many cases it is a question of "like mother, like daughter"! "Like father, like son"! This is called the law of "Generational Blessing, and Generational Iniquity" both of which we will look at in more detail in a moment.

There are a number of laws which are written into God's universe. These are decrees which God has intended to be used for our good, in order that we may be a blessed people who will live happy and fruitful lives. However, they are also laws which, if we withstand or disobey them, may also be used for our ill, especially if we do not fulfil their conditions. For example, one of the most important laws in God's universe is the **Law of Blessing and Curse**.

In Deuteronomy chapter 28, we are told all about God's

promises of blessing if we obey His commandments. These blessings are many and bounteous and include fruitfulness, health and a long life. God intends that these blessings will pass down the family line, so that not only will **we** be blessed, but our children will be blessed also. He promises us that:

> *"The righteous man walks in his integrity;*
> *His children are blessed after him."*   (Proverbs 20:7)

People in the natural world, of course, are very aware of the good things which come down the family line, for they will often remark that "Mary" is just like her grandpa, especially in the area of creativity, and that she also shows a remarkable likeness to her mother's sister. You will hear them comment on the fact that "John" is just like his father, very musical and excellent on the piano. They will even note and remark on the truth, that "Ruth" is just like her grandmother, delightful in nature, full of fun but with a strong and determined spirit! In fact they may even mention, that being a redhead like her great grandmother, she has also inherited that lady's fiery temper, as well as her warm and independent nature!

Christians are also very much aware of the blessings which are passed from one age to another; all of the good things, both material and spiritual, which are transferred down the generational line. For example, we can see the pattern of faith being passed down the family line in the life of Paul's companion Timothy. We are told that Timothy inherited his faith from his mother and his grandmother.

> *"I call to remembrance the genuine faith that is in you, which dwelt*
> *first in your grandmother Lois and your mother Eunice."*
>   (2 Timothy 1:5)

One can just imagine the godly grandmother of Timothy praying so much for her grandchild and being delighted to see the faithfulness of God, as He brings him to the place of like faith.

We also see the mercy of God coming down the generation line:

> *"Therefore know that the Lord your God, He is God, the faithful God who keeps covenant and mercy for a thousand generations with those who love Him and keep His commandments."*
>
> (Deuteronomy 7:9)

As, of course, does God's righteousness:

> *"But the mercy of the Lord is from everlasting to everlasting*
> *On those who fear Him,*
> *And His righteousness to children's children,*
> *To such as keep His covenant*
> *And to those who remember His commandments to do them."*
>
> (Psalm 103:17–18)

As well as the law of blessing there is also, written into God's universe, the **Law of Multiplication**. This is linked to the law of blessing, in that our God is a bountiful God, and He means those blessings to be multiplied from generation to generation. So He wrote into the universe His plan for the multiplication of good things. Referring to animals and birds He said:

> *"And God blessed them, saying, 'Be fruitful and multiply, and fill the waters in the seas, and let birds multiply on the earth.'"*
>
> (Genesis 1:22)

Whilst referring to mankind His word was:

> *"Then God blessed them, and God said to them, 'Be fruitful and multiply; fill the earth and subdue it.'"*   (Genesis 1:28)

God's multiplication flows out of God's abundant heart, for He desires to bless and be a blessing to His people throughout the generations. Therefore we see that His plan of multiplication is intricately linked into His plan of blessing. Peter and Jude knew the truth of this as we hear them praying for fellow Christians:

> *"Grace and peace be multiplied to you."*   (2 Peter 1:2)

> *"Mercy, peace, and love be multiplied to you."*   (Jude 1:2)

The disciples are very much aware that the blessings of peace, grace, love and mercy are not to be given meagrely by God, but instead He will shower them down upon His people according to His law of multiplication.

However, the plans of God are also linked into another one of God's laws, which is called the **Law of Sowing and Reaping**. Scripture tells us that if we sow upright actions, good habits, righteous attitudes and principles into our family line, then God will cause us to reap those things a thousand fold, for the multiplication factor comes into effect again. Nevertheless, God's law of sowing and reaping also includes the element of **justice**, for it is based on the principle of "whatsoever" we sow into our families (whether it is good or bad), that is what we will reap.

> *"Do not be deceived, God is not mocked; for whatsoever a man sows, that he will also reap.*   (Galatians 6:7)

Sin always has its consequences, and if we are in any doubt about that, we only have to consider the experiences of the nation of Israel. Speaking to the Israelite people God says:

"Sow for yourselves righteousness;
Reap in mercy;
Break up your fallow ground,
For it is time to seek the Lord,
Till He comes and rains righteousness on you.
You have ploughed wickedness;
You have reaped iniquity." (Hosea 10:12–13)

Thus, as well as blessings, we see that sinful actions and thoughts can also pass down the family line. This of course, is a distortion of God's original intention of passing multiplied benefits from one generation to another. This may result in illness, curses. and mental and emotional disturbances repeating themselves constantly in the family structure. So the sowing may be either good or bad. It can be a present-day sowing or one that was sown way back in the generational line. The effects of sin may also be out of all proportion to the sowing; thus we see the multiplication factor coming into fulfilment again. Hosea 8:7 says:

"They sow the wind, and reap the whirlwind."

There is an interesting story recorded in Judges chapter 1, concerning the war between Judah and Simeon, and the Canaanites. It tells the story of the king of that country, Adoni-Bezek, and relates how Judah and Simeon cut off his thumbs and big toes. Adoni-Bezek, in a moment of enlightenment recalls that:

15

> *"Seventy kings with their thumbs and big toes cut off used to gather their food under my table; as I have done, so God has repaid me."*
>
> (Judges 1:7)

This is a remarkable example of the law of sowing and reaping being at work within God's universe, for what Adoni-Bezek sowed, he also reaped. Here we find that he suffered the very same punishment as he had inflicted upon those seventy kings: his thumbs and toes were also truncated.

I am reminded of a lady I prayed for, who (to the surprise of both of us) was certainly carrying the grief from a great number of abortions, which had taken place in her generational line. The descendant was reaping the consequences of her parents' and her grandparents' sins.

Whilst the multiplication factor does come into effect in this law of sowing and reaping, nevertheless God in His mercy, has limited the consequences of the father's sins to three and four generations, whilst the law of blessing goes on for thousands!

> *"And the Lord passed before him and proclaimed, 'The Lord, the Lord God, merciful and gracious, longsuffering, and abounding in goodness and truth, keeping mercy for thousands, forgiving iniquity and transgression and sin, by no means clearing the guilty; visiting the iniquity of the fathers upon the children and the children's children to the third and the fourth generation."* (Exodus 34:6–7)

The writer of Deuteronomy confirms the consequences of sin:

> *"Then the Lord will bring upon you and your descendants extraordinary plagues – great and prolonged plagues – and prolonged sicknesses."*
>
> (Deuteronomy 28:59)

It is interesting to note that the writer reiterates that it is also the descendants who will suffer the consequences of the father's sin. Thus we find that the law of sowing and reaping, whilst linking in to the law of blessing, also links in with another law in God's universe, and that is the **Law of Generational Iniquity**.

The important question would seem to be, "What do we mean by generational iniquity?" The word itself is used in a number of scriptures, and in the context of the Ten Commandments, as recorded in Exodus 20:5, we hear God saying:

> *"I, the Lord your God, am a jealous God, visiting the iniquity of the fathers on the children to the third and fourth generations of those who hate me."*

What then does the word "iniquity" mean? In order to consider the meaning of the word "iniquity" it may help us to look at some of the other words, which are used for "sin" within the Scriptures. The word "**sin**" (*hamartia*) occurs over two hundred and fifty times in the New Testament and has the root idea, of falling short; an error; a failure; an independence of God. The word "**transgression**" (*parabasis*) carries with it the meaning of the breaking of a specific rule or law. The word "**trespass**" (*paraptoma*) means going onto forbidden territory; going where you shouldn't in spite of warnings and notices.

The word "**iniquity**" (*avon*) is used in many passages in the Old Testament (including Exodus 20:5), and carries the meaning of "perversity" and according to the New King James Version the word "iniquity" (*anomia*) as recorded in the New Testament, literally means "lawlessness". So the word has within it the idea of some sin or sins, resulting from a wrong desire, lawlessness, or a perverseness, which then causes a weakness and a compulsion in the make-up of our descendants or in us as a result of the sins of our ancestors.

The commentator C.J. Ellicott DD writes:

> "All history shows that this is a law of God's moral government of the world."

The fact is, that when our ancestors sin, there is the possibility of the consequence of their sin falling upon us. We are then vulnerable to sinning in the same areas and so compounding the problem for our children in the family line.

Exodus 20:5 says that if the people disobey the Ten Commandments (the Law) then the Lord will visit the iniquities of the fathers upon the children to the third and fourth generation. This results in a **flaw – a weakness, and a tendency to sin in that particular area by the family**. Like a **flaw** in a rock, so the initial sin introduces a tendency towards breaking the Law in the same area as the original sin. Leviticus chapter 26 hammers this message home:

> *"And those of you who are left shall waste away in their iniquity in your enemies' lands; also in their fathers' iniquities, which are with them, they shall waste away."* (Leviticus 26:39)

Jeremiah, whom many people believe wrote the book of Lamentations, writes:

> *"Our fathers sinned and are no more,*
> *But we bear their iniquities."* (Lamentations 5:7)

And in case we are in any doubt, the writer of Deuteronomy says that the Lord will be:

"... visiting the iniquity of the fathers upon the children to the third and fourth generation." (Deuteronomy 5:9)

Jeremiah picks up the theme again in the book named after him and asserts that:

"You show lovingkindness to thousands, and repay the iniquity of the fathers into the bosom of their children after them."

(Jeremiah 32:18)

Chapter 2

Some Common Objections to Generational Iniquity

What about the **sour grapes**?

> "In those days they shall say no more:
>   'The fathers have eaten sour grapes,
>   And the children's teeth are set on edge.'"   (Jeremiah 31:29)

Ezekiel, the prophet, quotes the same proverb as Jeremiah and some people might well legitimately ask the question, "What about Ezekiel chapter 18 and Jeremiah chapter 31. Where do they fit in with the view of generational iniquity?" These chapters refer to the fact that each man shall bear the consequences of his **own** sin. According to the commentator C.J. Ellicott DD, these chapters were written in the context of judgement and he carefully points out that both of the prophets are keen to stress that there is, and must be, a place for individual responsibility.

Both Jeremiah and Ezekiel are writing to people who were inclined to blame their own sins on the sins of their fathers. They evaded their own personal responsibility, and so both of the prophets want to bring home to them the stark truth that God will judge each man for his own sin. People were finding in the words of Exodus 20:5 an excuse for their own personal sin, rather than seeing it as a warning against passing on the weakness to their children.

C.J. Ellicott DD emphasises that the law of generational iniquity leaves untouched the freedom of man's free will. In this context he writes:

> "Thus it is true that God does both visit the sins of the fathers upon the children and at the same time does, through all, punish and reward each single person according to their own individual bearing towards Him."

He also states:

> "Individual suffering is certainly the consequence of individual sin . . . but these consequences are often slow in their development and may not fall upon the individual who has done the wrong, but upon some more or less remote descendants."

Thus we see that there is room in the Scriptures for both man's freedom of choice as to whether to sin or not, and also the fact that the sins of the fathers are visited upon the children to the third and fourth generation. One does not exclude the other; neither does one excuse the other, for both are valid.

Another common objection is the view that we are now under a **New Covenant** and therefore the Old Covenant is null and void. It is certainly true that we are under a New Covenant with the coming of the Lord Jesus Christ and His death upon the Cross. I hope to show in a later chapter the full benefits of the New Covenant, which Jesus has won for us. However, I would simply remind the reader that the New does not dispense with the Old, for as Jesus pointed out:

"Do not think that I came to destroy the Law or the Prophets. I did not come to destroy but to fulfill. For assuredly, I say to you, till heaven and earth pass away, one jot or one tittle will by no means pass from the law till all is fulfilled." (Matthew 5:17–18)

It is also very important for us to realise that just as we go to the Cross to appropriate for ourselves forgiveness for our own personal sin, so in a like manner we need to go to the Cross to appropriate what Jesus has won for us, in the removal of our family sin. We need to walk in the full benefits of the New Covenant, rather than knowing freedom in part, whilst still carrying around the weakness of our family iniquity. If it is correct that:

"You shall know the truth, and the truth shall set you free," (John 8:32)

then the more knowledge we have of what is entailed in the New Covenant, the more possible it is to walk in the truth of it, and therefore claim the benefits entailed and walk in its blessing.

Another common objection might be, "But it is so unfair, why should I suffer because of what some unknown ancestor did or did not do?" The observation is true, in that it is so obviously unfair, but once Adam and Eve had sinned, unfortunately they introduced unfairness into the system. The laws of God are neutral and are based on obedience and blessing, and the unfairness began because of man's sin. As we have seen already, the laws of God work for either good or ill, since these laws are just and unbiased. The wonder of it is, is that God in His mercy and through His Grace, found a way through the work of the Lord Jesus Christ, to redeem man and to provide the means for the iniquity to be stopped on the Cross.

Chapter 3

Biblical Evidence of Generational Iniquity – Sexual Sin

Two of the most basic questions would seem to be:

- "Does Scripture bear out the evidence of generational iniquity?"
- "Do the families, as depicted in the Bible, show that the pattern of sin; the breaking of God's law in a particular area; the tendency to sin in the same way, continues repeatedly down the family line?"

According to Exodus 20:14 the Lord commands us:

> *"You shall not commit adultery."*

Usually, adultery is a description of a married person having sexual intercourse outside of marriage. However, in the margin of the Amplified Bible, adultery is described as sexual sin in the widest sense. The writer asserts:

> "Observe here the expansion of the meaning of the seventh commandment in many catechisms to include whoredom in all its forms, as well as unchastity 'premarital relations, sexual

impurity, and lustful desire under whatever name.' (J.P. Lange, *A Commentary*). 'Not only is adultery forbidden here, but also fornication and all kinds of mental and sensual uncleanness. All impure books, songs, pictures etc., which tend to inflame and debauch the mind are against this law.' (Adam Clarke, *The Holy Bible* with a Commentary)"

In the context of sexual sin it is interesting to observe how the pattern of immorality is repeated generation after generation in the family line of King David. He was a descendant of the line of Judah, who was the son of Jacob and Rachel. Judah had intercourse, inadvertently, with his daughter-in-law, Tamar. In Genesis chapter 38, we read the story of the incestuous relationship between them, and even though it was unintentional on Judah's part, nevertheless he introduced into his family line a tendency to sin in this particular way. According to Deuteronomy chapter 27 there is a curse which will come upon those who commit incest and this curse will pass down the family line. Leviticus, chapter 18 also warns against sexual sin and its consequences and in verse 15 we read:

> *"You shall not uncover the nakedness of your daughter-in-Jaw – she is your son's wife – you shall not uncover her nakedness."*

Judah, through his intercourse with Tamar, exposed her nakedness and the fruit of their union were twin boys, Zerah and Perez. As we consider the family line of Perez we see that the same weakness, the same flaw, the same tendency to sin in the sexual area is passed down the generational line.

There were ten generations between Judah and King David, the book of Ruth 4:18–22 gives the genealogy of Perez's family line. God normally restricted the sins of the fathers to three or four generations, but for sexual sin we read in Deuteronomy chapter 23 that it was to be for ten generations.

"One of illegitimate birth shall not enter the congregation of the Lord; even to the tenth generation none of his descendants shall enter the congregation of the Lord." (Deuteronomy 23:2)

It is very interesting to note that King David's son, Amnon, also has an incestuous relationship with his half-sister, who is also called Tamar. In the King James Version of the Bible, 2 Samuel chapter 13 is entitled "Incest in David's House", but in actuality the incest had been in his house from the original sin of Judah and his daughter-in-law Tamar. In a very real sense, whilst King David and his son Amnon were very much responsible for their own sins they were also walking in the sins of their fathers.

In this sphere of sexual sin, we can also see the sin of abuse within marriage being passed down the family line. Three generations of Abraham's family abuse their relationship with their wives, Abraham being the one to introduce the weakness, and the flaw into the line.

Abraham Opens Sarah up to Possible Abuse

In Genesis 12:10–20 we have the story of Abraham travelling south because of a famine in the land in which they were living. As they approach Egypt, Abraham says to Sarah:

"Indeed I know that you are a woman of beautiful countenance. Therefore it will happen, when the Egyptians see you, that they will say, 'This is his wife'; and they will kill me, but they will let you live. Please say that you are my sister, that it may be well with me for your sake, and that I may live because of you." (Genesis 12:11–13)

Abraham's abuse of Sarah lay in the fact that he removed his protection from her and opened her up to the possibility of committing sexual sin outside of her marriage.

God judged the situation very severely and sent plagues upon the house of Pharaoh. However, in Genesis chapter 20, we see Abraham repeating his sin, but this time he doesn't ask Sarah to lie for him, instead he lies himself:

> "'She is my sister.' And Abimelech king of Gerar sent and took Sarah."
> (Genesis 20:2)

Abraham was playing on the fact that she was indeed his half-sister, but we see that again he was opening his wife up to possible abuse. God judged that sin also, and in His mercy He protected both Sarah and Abraham by warning Abimelech in a dream and saying to him:

> "Indeed you are a dead man because of the woman whom you have taken, for she is a man's wife."
> (Genesis 20:3)

And God again closed the wombs of the women in his house. It is interesting to see that He allowed Abraham to pray for healing for the women and God heard his prayer,

> " . . . and God healed Abimelech, his wife, and his maidservants. Then they bore children."
> (Genesis 20:17)

Isaac Opens Rebekah up to Possible Abuse

The consequence of Abraham's sin was that the tendency to sin in the same area – the "flaw", the iniquity – was passed onto his son Isaac:

"So Isaac dwelt in Gerar. And the men of the place asked him about his wife. And he said, 'She is my sister'; for he was afraid to say, 'She is my wife,' because he thought, 'lest the men of the place should kill me for Rebekah, because she is beautiful to behold.'"

(Genesis 26:6–7)

Just like his father, Isaac opened his wife, Rebekah, up to possible abuse, for we see here that Isaac repeats his father's sin! The consequence of Isaac's sin and the iniquity – the "flaw", the weakness – was passed on to his son Jacob.

Jacob Opens Leah up to Possible Abuse

Jacob repeats his father's and his grandfather's sin but in a different way. The tendency – the flaw – comes out in a slightly altered manner, but nevertheless we can see his abuse of his wife, Leah. Jacob had been deceived by Laban and had been given Leah as his wife instead of Rachel her sister, whom he loved. He did not love Leah, at least in the beginning, and yet he had continual sexual intercourse with her. The names of her children give a vivid description of how Leah must have felt.

"When the Lord saw that Leah was unloved, He opened her womb; but Rachel was barren. So Leah conceived and bore a son, and she called his name Reuban; for she said, 'The Lord has surely looked on my affliction. Now therefore, my husband will love me.'"

(Genesis 29:31–32)

The word "unloved" is literally translated "hated". Imagine having a sexual relationship with someone who hates you! The names of each of the children who followed spoke of Leah's abuse and misery. Her second son she called, Simeon, meaning:

27

"Because the Lord has heard that I am unloved."   (Genesis 29:33)

Her third son she named Levi:

"Now this time my husband will become attached to me, because I have borne him three sons."   (Genesis 29:34)

She is desperately trying to buy her husband's affection and protection. Leah goes on to have another child whom she names Judah, because she affirms *"Now I will praise the Lord."* One feels that Leah has won through to a place of contentment and peace, with or without her husband's help. Jacob's sin was that he had sexual relationships with his wife whilst hatred was filling his heart. He used her for his own ends. He was repeating his father's and his grandfather's sin! We note here that indeed the sins of the fathers are visited upon the children, to the third and fourth generation, and to ten generations for sexual sin.

In the same family we see another weakness being passed down the family line, which, whilst it is not the same sin, is connected with it: that of dishonouring and deception. For linked into Abraham, Isaac and Jacob's abuse of their wives there was a strong thread of not honouring the wives whom God had given to them and also the willingness to deceive other people.

Chapter 4

Biblical Evidence of Generational Iniquity – Dishonouring and Deception

Jacob Dishonours and Deceives Isaac

In Exodus 20:12 God commands that people should:

> *"Honour your father and your mother that your days may be long upon the land."*

In Genesis chapter 27, we see Jacob being willing to dishonour and deceive his father Isaac, at his mother's instigation, by pretending to be Esau, and receive the blessing as the firstborn. Esau, of course, when he finds out is devastated, as also is Isaac, his father, for we hear him crying out:

> *"Your brother came with deceit and has taken away your blessing."*
> (Genesis 27:35)

At that moment, a dishonouring of parents and a disposition to deception entered the family line. The weakness and the flaw were to continue for a number of generations.

It is very interesting to see that Jacob deceived and dishonoured his father (with his mother's help) by the use of two young goats. They killed them and used their skin for the clothing of Jacob's arms. Rebekah was totally involved in the deception:

> *"And she put the skins of the kids of the goats on his hands and on the smooth part of his neck."* (Genesis 27:16)

Jacob's Sons Deceive Him

It is enlightening to see the way in which Jacob's sons inherit and pass on their father's sin. For they too, in turn, dishonour and deceive him! The sin, iniquity, and weakness are passed on. It is interesting too, to see that they also use a goatskin in their deception! The brothers of Joseph, Jacob's favourite son, sell Joseph to the Ishmaelites, because they are jealous of the attention which he continually receives from their father. They dishonour their father by being willing to deceive him and in order to do this we read:

> *"So they took Joseph's tunic, killed a kid of the goats, and dipped the tunic in the blood. Then they sent the tunic of many colours, and they brought it to their father and said, 'We have found this. Do you know whether it is your son's tunic or not?'"* (Genesis 37:31–32)

They, too, make use of a kid of a goat.

Ham Dishonours His Father

There is an interesting story in Genesis chapter 9, concerning the family of Noah and his son Ham who dishonours his father through sexual perversion. One evening Noah got drunk and lay naked in his tent. Ham looked into the tent and saw his father's nakedness. On doing so he should have covered his father over and closed the opening of the tent to protect his father's honour, but instead he called out to his brothers Shem and Japheth to "come and have a look." Thus he dishonoured his father, for it was strictly forbidden:

> *"None of you shall approach anyone who is near of kin to him, to uncover his nakedness."* (Leviticus 18:6)

Shem and Japheth were more honouring of their father, for they went in backward and covered Noah up.

Ham's Sexual Sin Grows and Expands

However, in Ham's family line the sin, the iniquity, the weakness is passed on, for we see that Ham's descendants followed in their father's footsteps! When God was bringing the children of Israel into the land of Canaan (the descendants of Ham) He gave them strict instructions not to behave as the Canaanites do, for He says:

> *"I visit the punishment of its iniquity upon it."* (Leviticus 18:25)

The warning, which He gives to the children of Israel, is in the whole context of sexual sin and sexual perversion. The original sin of Ham was that he dishonoured his father through his sexual depravity of looking on his father's nakedness. Thus his voyeurism introduced a weakness, a flaw, a tendency into his generational line, which multiplied and expanded in his descendants, so that eventually it included bestiality, homosexuality and incest as well. Truly it could be said of Ham and his descendants:

> *"The land is defiled."*   (Leviticus 18:25)

It is sobering to think that so much sin sprang from one man sinning and thus he introduced the weakness into his family line.

Chapter 5

Biblical Evidence of Generational Iniquity – Murder in the Family Line

In the context of the Ten Commandments, and therefore in the context of generational iniquity, the law states:

> *"You shall not commit murder."*   (Exodus 20:13)

Cain and Lamech

Looking at the family line of Cain, who murdered his brother Abel, we see that having introduced violence into his family line, his descendants suffer the consequences of his sin. His generational descendants are described in Genesis 4:16–24. One of Cain's descendants, Lamech, writes,

> *"For I have killed a man for wounding me,*
> *Even a young man for hurting me.*
> *If Cain shall be avenged sevenfold,*
> *Then Lamech seventy-sevenfold."*   (Genesis 4:23–24)

When God warned Cain, before he murdered his brother that:

> *" . . . sin lies at the door. And its desire is for you, but you should rule over it,"*   (Genesis 4:7)

one gets the feeling that when Cain sinned he opened a generational door of murder and violence that continued to affect his generational line for many years. The iniquity, the "flaw", in this instance, as with the sexual perversion of Ham, has passed down the line and grown in intensity, and we see Lamech almost boasting of his violent behaviour.

Esau and Jacob

In this area of murder and violence we can see the patterns of sin being repeated in the life of Esau and Jacob. We have already noted that Jacob stole Esau's blessing, and as a result hatred grew in Esau's heart.

> *"So Esau hated Jacob because of the blessing with which his father blessed him, and Esau said in his heart, 'The days of mourning for my father are at hand; then I will kill my brother Jacob.'"*
>
> (Genesis 27:41)

Here began a feud that was to cost countless lives throughout the history of the Israelite people, for Esau's descendants did much killing and were known as a very violent and vindictive people. Indeed his family, the Edomites, became known throughout the nation as a vengeful and warlike people. Ezekiel chapter 25 talks of the Edomites as being a very revengeful people and in Ezekiel chapter 35, God gave a description of their end. Speaking judgement on them He says:

> *"'Because you have had an ancient hatred, and have shed the blood of the children of Israel by the power of the sword at the time of their calamity, when their iniquity came to an end, therefore, as I live,' says*

34

the Lord God, 'I will prepare you for blood, and blood shall pursue you.'" (Ezekiel 35:5–6)

This was a horrifying judgement to descend upon Esau's family line, all springing from Esau's hatred in his heart for his brother Jacob. It is interesting to note that Esau did not kill his brother, but nevertheless he had determined to do so in his heart. It reminds us of the words of Jesus:

"You have heard that it was said to those of old, 'You shall not murder,' and whoever murders will be in danger of the judgement. But I say to you that whoever is angry with his brother shall be in danger of the judgement." (Matthew 5:21–22)

Murder of the Gibeonites

In this sphere of generational iniquity there is a very interesting story recorded in 2 Samuel chapter 21. Way back in Israel's history, Joshua had made a covenant with the Gibeonites. They had deceived him, by pretending to be from a far country and from a destitute people (Joshua 9). Joshua and the leadership had neglected to take counsel of the Lord and thus made a covenant with the Gibeonites, which had they sought the Lord, they could have been saved from. Nevertheless, Joshua was a man of his word and he had made a promise before God that he would care for them and protect them and to the best of his knowledge he did just that.

However, in King David's time there was a famine in the land, and David inquired of the Lord as to why this was so?

"And the Lord answered, 'It is because of Saul and his bloodthirsty house, because he killed the Gibeonites.'" (2 Samuel 21:1)

God had brought judgement on the land of Israel because Saul had not kept the covenant which Joshua had made with the Gibeonites, but instead had slain them. King David went to the Gibeonites and asked them what they wanted?

> *"'Let seven men of his descendants be delivered to us, and we will hang them before the Lord in Gibeah of Saul, whom the Lord chose.' And the king said, 'I will give them.'"* (2 Samuel 21:6)

Seven of Saul's descendants died in payment for Saul's sin, surely an instance of the children suffering for the sins of their fathers. It was only after the debt was paid that the famine was lifted.

> *"And after that God heeded the prayer for the land."*
>
> (2 Samuel 21:14)

Jesus' Strong Words

In Matthew 23:29–32, Jesus makes some very interesting comments in this whole area of generational iniquity. He makes reference to the fact that the scribes and Pharisees are the:

> *" . . . sons of those who murdered the prophets."* (Matthew 23:31)

He is referring to the murder of the prophets and the servants of God throughout Jewish history. He asserts that the scribes and Pharisees are tainted with their murder:

> *"That on you may come all the righteous blood shed on the earth, from the blood of righteous Abel to the blood of Zechariah, son of Berechiah, whom **you murdered** between the temple and the altar."*
>
> (Matthew 23:35)

36

The reference *"Abel to . . . Zechariah"* would indicate to the Jewish people that Jesus was including the whole of the Scriptures. This accusation *"whom you murdered"* can only be understood in the light of generational iniquity. For these scribes and Pharisees were not actually alive at the time of the murders, although they were showing all the signs that they carried the flaw, the weaknesses of their fathers.

Chapter 6

Biblical Evidence of Generational Iniquity – Idolatry in the Family Line

According to Exodus 20:4–5 we are expressly forbidden to worship idols, and it is in especial reference to this that the Lord talks about visiting the sins of the fathers upon the children.

> *"You shall not make for yourself any carved image, or any likeness of anything that is in heaven above, or that is in the earth beneath, or that is in the water under the earth; you shall not bow down to them nor serve them. For I, the Lord your God am a jealous God, visiting the iniquity of the fathers on the children to the third and fourth generations of those who hate me."*   (Exodus 20:4–5)

In the worship of Molech, as referred to in Leviticus 20:1–5, God says that not only will He punish those who worship idols, He will also bring punishment upon those who compromise with the false worshipper. So serious is the sin of idol worship.

> *"And if the people of the land should in any way hide their eyes from the man, when he gives some of his descendants to Molech, and they do not kill him, then I will set my face against that man and against his family."*   (Leviticus 20:4–5)

False worship is like a root, which if left undealt with, will grow and spread into a bitter and poisonous plant.

"So that there may not be among you man or woman or family or tribe, whose heart turns away today from the Lord our God, to go and serve the gods of these nations, and that there may not be among you a root bearing bitterness or wormwood." (Deuteronomy 29:18)

Idolatry had the serious potential of spreading throughout the generations like a canker, which is why God spoke to strongly against it, and the history of Israel proves the great dangers inherent in it. The family of Israel's kings is an amazing illustration of a family who turned towards the worship of idols and thus brought upon themselves the words of Exodus 20:4–5.

There are some very interesting people in the family line of King David and his son, King Solomon. It is salutary that it was King Solomon himself who introduced idolatry into the family line:

"For it was so, when Solomon was old, that his wives turned his heart after other gods; and his heart was not loyal to the Lord his God, as was the heart of his father David." (1 Kings 11:4)

After Solomon's death the kingdom was divided into two: Israel and Judah, which was due to the foolishness of his son Rehoboam (1 Kings 12). All of the kings of Israel *"did evil in the sight of the Lord"* (1 Kings 15:34), and eventually they were taken into captivity. King Ahab was part of this line, as was his father Omri who

" . . . did evil in the eyes of the Lord, and did worse than all who were before him." (1 Kings 16:25)

However, because the line of Judah is the family line of Jesus we will consider and concentrate on those kings and their generational line. Reading the history of Judah, you will notice that every now and again there is a good king who tries to re-establish the worship of Jehovah. Nevertheless, mixed in with them, there often arises a king who continues to practise idolatry as Solomon did, when he took foreign wives and took their idolatry on board at the same time, introducing it into the family line.

The history as recorded in 1 Kings 14–23, makes very interesting reading as regards the teaching of generational iniquity and how the Lord continues to keep someone on the throne with the same heart as King David. The following kings were such men: Asa, Jehoshaphat, Hezekiah and Josiah. It was often written concerning them that:

> " . . . he did what was right in the sight of the Lord, according to all
> that his father David had done."   (2 Kings 18:3)

In this instance the writer was referring to King Hezekiah, truly a man like King David, for he was a man after God's own heart. It is interesting however to see how the weakness and the flaw keeps resurrecting itself within the family, for Hezekiah's son, Manasseh, was the exact opposite of his father. He introduced terrible and wicked practices (as recorded in 2 Kings chapter 21) amongst the people of Judah.

In this area of idolatry, there is also included the sin of worshipping false religions as well as dabbling in any forbidden occult activity. King Manasseh was involved in all of these things. He raised up altars to Baal, he worshipped Assyrian gods, and he profaned the house of the Lord by building altars to false gods within them.

> *"Also he made his son pass through the fire, practised soothsaying, used witchcraft, and consulted spiritists and mediums. He did much evil in the sight of the Lord, to provoke Him to anger."*
>
> (2 Kings 21:6)

Such things would bring the curse of God both upon the person involved, and on his family also, as we will see in the next chapter.

Chapter 7

The Power of the Curse

In the first chapter, I made reference to the law of "blessing and curse" as recorded in Deuteronomy chapter 28, and how God's intention was that those blessings would pass down the family line. These would be given in response to people being obedient to God's laws. In the same chapter we have reference to what happens if we disobey His commandments and the terrible consequence of curse which will follow:

> *"But it shall come to pass, if you do not obey the voice of the Lord your God, to observe carefully all His commandments and His statutes which I command you today, that all these curses will come upon you and overtake you."* (Deuteronomy 28:15)

We need to always remember that the reason why God places a curse, is in order to bring a person or a family under judgement and therefore to a place where they can receive His mercy and forgiveness. This, hopefully, will eventually lead them to confession, repentance, forgiveness and freedom.

Having ascertained God's purposes in bringing a curse upon a person, let us look at a few of the specific curses, as recorded in Deuteronomy chapter 27; looking at what they are, how they are given; and in what way they work within the family line.

Curses Passed Down the Line

As we have seen, the main reason for God's curse falling upon a person and his family is in response to their disobedience and the breaking of His laws, that is the Ten Commandments.

> *"And they [the curses] shall be upon you for a sign and a wonder, and on your descendants forever."* (Deuteronomy 28:46)

False Religions, Occult, Idolatry, Worship of Other Gods

As we have seen, any worship of foreign gods invokes the wrath of the true and living God.

> *"Cursed is the one who makes any carved or moulded image, an abomination to the Lord."* (Deuteronomy 27:15)

This false worship would include being involved with any religion that denies the humanity and the divinity of the Lord Jesus Christ: for example, Jehovah's Witnesses, Freemasonry, Spiritualism, Christian Science, etc.

Dishonouring of Parents

To dishonour parents is a very serious sin in the eyes of the Lord, for they are the ones who are intended to input the true "fear of the Lord" into the child and to "raise him up in the way in which he should go." Therefore God speaks a curse on anyone who dishonours his or her mother and father.

> *"Cursed is the one who treats his father or mother with contempt."* (Deuteronomy 27:16)

Injustice and Oppression

Injustice and oppression is a great abomination to the Lord, for His heart is for the underdog, for those who have no one to stand up for their cause. He especially has a heart for the weak or the helpless and God is very much against the man or woman who rides upon their backs for their own advancement. Deuteronomy 27:17–19 talk about the various unjust situations which will bring God's curse upon a person and his descendants. These include the orphan, the foreigner and the woman without a husband:

> *"Cursed is the one who perverts the justice due the stranger, the fatherless, and the widow."*   (Deuteronomy 27:19)

Sexual Sin

As we have seen, any sexual sin brings consequences upon the family line, but here in Deuteronomy we are told that it actually also brings a curse upon the person and the family.

> *"Cursed is the one who lies with his father's wife."*
> (Deuteronomy 27:20)

> *"Cursed is the one who lies with any kind of animal."*
> (Deuteronomy 27:21)

> *"Cursed is the one who lies with his sister."*
> (Deuteronomy 27:22)

> *"Cursed is the one who lies with his mother-in-law."*
> (Deuteronomy 27:23)

Here we see that bestiality, incest, and sexual perversion all bring a curse upon the person and his generational line.

Stealing and Lying

In this area of curse, there are some very interesting verses in Zechariah 5:1–4. Referring to thieves and robbers God says:

> "'I will send out the curse,' says the Lord of hosts;
> 'It shall enter the house of the thief
> And the house of the one who swears falsely by My name.
> It shall remain in the midst of his house
> And consume it, with its timber and stones.'" (Zechariah 5:4)

The word "house" in Hebrew really means, "the family, the structure", and in fact everything concerned with the person. There have been a number of times when we have prayed with people around their houses because they have sensed that there may be a curse at work. As they have confessed and repented of anything ungodly which may have gone on in the past, so there has come a lightening and a cleansing of the atmosphere within the house.

The Curse of Words

As well as God, a person can also put a curse upon another, and in this area words are very powerful indeed. Especially powerful are the words of any authority figures, for example the words of a **spouse** can go very deep, and in this context I find the words of Jacob to his wife Rachel very interesting. Rachel stole some family idols from her father's house; this was a sin in itself, of course, and a sin that would have brought a curse upon her and her descendants. When her father, Laban, is searching for the family idols, Jacob virtually curses his wife with the words:

"'With whomever you find your gods, do not let him live. In the presence of our brethren, identify what I have of yours and take it with you.' For Jacob did not know that Rachel had stolen them."

(Genesis 31:32)

It is informative that Rachel had already brought herself under God's curse by worshipping false images. It is also interesting that in order to hide the idols, she proceeded to sit upon them. The place where she hid the false gods, became the place of her death, for it was as she brought forth her child from her womb, past the place where she had put the idols, that Rachel died. She either had, or pretended to have, her monthly period, therefore there would appear to be a direct connection between the hiding of the false gods and the means of her death. There is a real power in the curse of words: "Do not let him live," says Jacob, probably never even realising that he was talking about Rachel, his wife.

Parents
A parent's words to a child are also very forceful as well as powerful and they can keep the children under a curse for months or even years, for it is very true that:

"Death and life are in the power of the tongue."   (Proverbs 18:21)

A baby can even hear the blessing or cursing of the words of his parents, as early as in the first few months whilst he or she is being formed within the womb. Luke 1:41 affirms that it was whilst John the Baptist was in the womb, that he responded to the words of Mary the mother of Jesus:

" . . . when Elizabeth heard the greeting of Mary, that the babe leaped in her womb."

46

Therefore if a baby hears such words of cursing as: "I hate this baby, it will never amount to anything;" "I don't want this child;" "I am going to get rid of this baby;" then that curse of words can have a long and a lasting effect. Until a certain age, parents are as God to a child and if our mothers or fathers have said to us in the past, "You're useless," "You're hopeless," "You're no good," "You're pathetic," "Nobody will ever want to marry you," then we probably will believe them. The words will go straight into our spirit and we may begin to live according to their expectation of us, and according to the curse which they have placed upon us.

If a parent has been exceedingly strict with a child, then their very strictness may put fear into them and this will be as an entrance door, which will allow their words to become like arrows penetrating their spirit and causing them to walk under the curse. One lady was labouring under the curse of her father, who happened to be a sergeant major both on the parade ground and at home. His voice held such power and authority over her that whatever he said, "must be true." His words were, "You are a disgrace to this family and you will be a shame to any other family which you might become a part of." She married in her early twenties, and for years lived under the curse of those words. Her husband was never able to understand why she continually apologised for both herself and their children.

Teachers
In this domain of curse of words, teachers are very important to the young child, for they take over the parent's authority to some extent. Their words can be for good or ill, and many a child will believe that if the teacher says it, then it must be true! I am reminded of the teacher who literally dragged a child out to the front of the class and made fun of him because he didn't

know his ten-times table. She was hoping to make an example of him, so that the other children would do their homework that night and pass their test the following morning. However, the words she used rang in that boy's ears until he was a grown man of thirty. "You are stupid, you'll never make anything of yourself." He was a bright boy, but he never did amount to anything – intellectually. He believed the teacher's pronouncements!

Church Leaders

The words of other authoritarian people are also very powerful and some leaders have abused their position and spoken words which have set people back for years in the Christian life, as have also the words of some **threatening figures**. A prime example would be that of **Jezebel** and her curse of words upon Elijah. After Elijah had called upon God on Mount Carmel to answer by fire, and had killed the prophets of Baal, Jezebel comes and threatens to take his life.

> *"And Ahab told Jezebel all that Elijah had done, also how he had executed all the prophets with the sword. Then Jezebel sent a messenger to Elijah, saying, 'So let the gods do to me, and more also, if I do not make your life as the life of one of them by tomorrow about this time.'"*
> (1 Kings 19:1–2)

Those words were enough to send Elijah into a spiral of despair, for they went straight into his spirit and totally crushed him. I believe that was why he ran off into the wilderness. Words are very powerful and they can crush, bruise and break the spirit, which is why the writer of Proverbs affirms that:

> *"Death and life are in are power of the tongue."* (Proverbs 18:21)

Abuser

Another threatening situation may be that of abuse, for abusers will very often put a curse of words upon a person whom they have abused, in order to keep them silent. This happened to Jane, a little girl who was bound into secrecy by her abuser for, "If you tell your mother she will be sent to prison." So strong was the curse of words, that even when she grew into womanhood, she found it impossible to share the deepest secrets of her heart with her husband and her family. However, not only did she suffer but also the whole family came under a cloud of secrecy. It is interesting to observe that James writes that,

> " . . . *the tongue is a fire, a world of iniquity. The tongue is so set among our members that it defiles the whole body, and sets on fire the course of nature; and it is set on fire by hell.*" (James 3:6)

Certainly in Jane's situation, her whole family was defiled and suffered the consequences of the abuser's sin. It is also possible of course, for a curse to be put upon a person from a number of other sources, which it is not in the remit of this book to consider, as we are simply looking at family weaknesses and curses as a result of family sin. However, there are some excellent books on the market, which give a fuller description of curses and their results.

Chapter 8

Indications of a Curse at Work

There will be several indications if a curse is at work within a person's life or within a family, one of which may be that **repeated sicknesses** can develop in the family line. In regards to the curses which will come on people for disobedience, Deuteronomy 28:59 affirms:

> *"then the Lord will bring upon you and your descendants extraordinary plagues – great and prolonged plagues – and serious and prolonged sicknesses."*

Some people's families struggle with continued infirmity; backaches, migraines, stomach trouble, etc., which may spring from many and varied sources. They could be purely physical or emotional in nature, but they also could be as a result of a curse at work within the family.

An illustration of such a curse is to be found in the very interesting story of Elisha and his servant Gehazi. In 2 Kings chapter 5 we have the incident which is recorded, of the time when God healed Naaman, a commander of the army of the King of Syria, of leprosy. Naaman had been so delighted with his healing, that as a token of thanks he had offered Elisha a gift, but Elisha had refused it because Naaman's healing was the work of God. Gehazi, Elisha's servant, did not have similar

principles and so he goes after Naaman and tells him that Elisha
has changed his mind. He then takes from Naaman some silver.
When he returns to Elisha, he receives a rebuke from Elisha
and these words:

> *"'Therefore the leprosy of Naaman shall cling to you and your
> descendants forever.' And he went out from his presence leprous, as
> white as snow."* (2 Kings 5:27)

Gehazi's generational line suffered the consequences of Gehazi's
sin.

Another clue that a curse may be at work within a family is
if there is a pattern of frequent **marriage breakdown** within
the generations. Maybe you see a pattern of divorce, separation,
or family discord in the generational line. We have prayed into
a number of marriages which had a curse put on them by one
of the sets of parents, even before the couple arrived at the altar!
"This marriage will never work." "You are totally incompatible,"
or as one father said to his daughter, "There will always be your
room ready, when you decide you have had enough." It has been
said that persistent opposition by parents to a marriage is closely
linked with marital breakdown, although the writer could not
understand the mechanism which was at work. He was not a
Christian. One would wonder if this were an example of a curse
of words being at work.

An atmosphere of **poverty**, if it were frequently repeated,
would appear to be a sign of a curse at work, and would always
be worth exploring as a possible cause. We have prayed with a
number of people who have had ancestors who have been free-
masons, only to find that repeated infirmity or poverty has been
a result within the person or their descendants when they have
left the lodge. The writer of Deuteronomy says:

"Cursed shall be your basket and your kneading bowl. Cursed shall be the fruit of your body and the produce of your land, the increase of your cattle and the offspring of your flocks."

(Deuteronomy 28:17–18)

A very descriptive picture of abject poverty, which you will notice, can also include the state of childlessness, although this is not necessarily the only reason for this condition.

A **proneness to accidents** may also indicate that there is a curse at work, linked in with a pattern of **early** or **untimely deaths**. One man, for whom we prayed, was ill with a kidney problem. His father had died at approximately the same age as our friend, which was in his early forties. Not only that, but his grandfather also died at the same age. It was almost too much of a coincidence. One man who was approaching his fifties said, "Something overtook my father's father when he was in his fifties, I am in my fifties, I feel rocked by waves of hundreds of years." He had a nervous breakdown shortly afterwards.

Of course, we need to remember that the reason why God places a curse upon a person, is in response to that person's sin and disobedience and it is there in order to bring that person or family under judgement. This will hopefully lead to their confession and repentance, as well as direct them towards forgiveness and freedom.

The way to deliverance from a curse is very similar to the way in which we would bring a person to freedom in any other area. First of all there needs to be a **confession** of faith in Jesus as the deliverer and the one who carried our curse for us on the Cross. Secondly, there needs to be **confession and repentance** for any sin in our own lives, or in the life of our ancestors, which has allowed the curse to find a landing place. We may know what that is, or we may simply need to take accountability for any family sin which has brought the curse into effect.

There will need to be **forgiveness** of the family for any sin which they have committed, and which has brought the consequences of the curse onto the family. The person for whom you are praying, will need to **renounce** all contact with the occult, false worship etc., depending on the reason for the curse coming into being, if this is known. The **prayer of release** is also vital, and a suggested prayer might be:

> *"Thank you Jesus for dying on the Cross to take my curse upon Yourself. I ask You now to release me from every curse that has been operating in my life because of my own, or my family's sin. By faith I receive that release and thank You for it in Jesus Name."*

Chapter 9

Modern Examples of Sin Travelling Down the Family Line

We have seen how generational iniquity travels down the family line within the families in Scripture, but the question now would seem to be: "Is there similar evidence that the same sin or weakness happens today?" A social worker that was sitting in on a teaching course which we were holding, confirmed to us that in the secular world they know all about generational iniquity. For him there was little doubt, for to them it is a fact of life that abuse, alcoholism, adultery, etc., often, although not inevitably, will run in families.

Sexual Sin

As we were teaching on this subject, a man who was at the seminar suddenly realised that he, his father, his grandfather and now his sons had all been involved with **molesting** young boys. Surprisingly, this gave him a great deal of hope, rather than adding to his despair, for he began to see a reason for his sin and for the family weakness which was so evident within himself and his sons. He also began to see the possibility of the sin and the iniquity, being dealt with at the Cross.

Another man, with whom we prayed, had begun **abusing**

girls when he was eleven years old. (The girl had approached him for a sexual relationship; she was around the age of twelve to thirteen at the time.) By the age of eighteen he had committed **incest** with his mother, and in his early twenties he had found out, to his great surprise and shame, that he was simply following in his father's footsteps. The pattern of his sin was almost an identical copy of his father's, who had also experienced intercourse with his own mother and had also indulged in a lifetime of affairs.

Mary was six years old when her uncle first began to abuse her, and for years she shared her guilty secret with no one. However, on sharing about the abuse with her mother much later in life, she was amazed to learn that not only had her mum been abused around the age of six, but so also had her maternal grandmother! Three generations of abuse, beginning at the same age – surely it was too much of a coincidence.

Alcohol and Adultery

Alcohol and adultery are fairly well-known patterns of behaviour, which can be observed as repeating patterns within families. Dr Bonnie Eaker Weil did some research into the subject of adultery, and affirms that she now believes that infidelity can be inherited. She also believes that knowledge of these patterns of adultery in a person's past can help the present-day couple avoid a break up. Writing in the *Daily Express* on Tuesday, 3 August, 1993 she says,

"At that moment I began to see that adultery – much like alcoholism or abuse – was a multi-generational thing."

She goes on,

"I've counselled more than 1,000 couples, 80 per cent because one or the other had been unfaithful. In nine out of ten cases, sometimes involving four generations with grandparents as well as parents and children, at least one partner was the adult child of an adulterer."

The same pattern can often be seen in the alcoholic and his descendants. We have observed a number of men, whose father and grandfather and now their sons have all walked the same path of being unable to resist drinking to excess. It is often when parents see the patterns being repeated in their children that they begin to look at their family line and yearn for release from the weakness and the flaw, which is not only blighting them but is now beginning to blight their children as well. The same pattern of family sin is, of course, sometimes seen in the drug abuser and his family.

Dishonouring Parents

Dishonouring parents can sometimes be seen travelling down the generational line as well. Maybe the parents will notice that there is an attitude of rebellion amongst their children, a putting down of the parents in front of others; in fact, they and others may remark that within the young people there is a standing against any authority and parental figures. This rebellion is usually in spite of there being some good and genuine discipline within the home.

Murder, Rage and Anger

Murder, rage and anger can also keep appearing within the family line. A man spoke to us fairly recently because he was troubled with outbursts of deep anger towards others who seemed to be a threat to him. This was eventually traced to his ancestry, which were the Scottish clans to which he belonged. His father, his grandfather and his great grandfather had all struggled with outbursts of rage. It was revealed, through his own research into the family history, that his great, great grandfather had murdered someone in one of the raids upon the English.

Stealing

Sometimes you will notice a tendency to steal or pilfer within a family – a tendency to take what is not yours. I am reminded of the story of Achan, as recorded in Scripture in the book of Joshua, chapter 7. Achan stole some accursed things, and this resulted in his family being put to death. He introduced the sin of stealing into his family line and all his family suffered retribution, but this time it was almost immediate. They reaped what Achan had sown!

An interesting story concerns a soldier who stole a medal from someone who was dead on the battlefield. It was reported that from that moment on his whole family began to have a problem with pilfering. The tendency to steal actually increased in intensity when the stolen medal was brought into the person's home.

Idolatry

A girl who was adopted by a Christian couple found herself drawn irresistibly towards the occult and into spiritualism. When they investigated the background of the birth mother they found out that she had been involved with many areas of the occult. It was revealed that the mother had used a Ouija board and had attempted suicide after it had spelt out the word "death" to her. The one area that this girl found most difficult to resist was the use of the Ouija board!

There could of course be a number of reasons why these patterns are repeated. For example, it may simply be that the children are raised in a family atmosphere of drugs or drink, etc., and they are picking up the family patterns. It may be that they are reaping the consequences of living in a dysfunctional family, and they are repeating the dysfunctional behaviour within their own families. There may be physical reasons for repeated patterns or infirmities, or it may be that the children are walking in the path of generational iniquity and are suffering the consequences of their father's sin and thus are following the pattern of "like father like son." It may also, of course, be that a "familiar spirit" is working through the generational weakness, and is enticing the children into the same sin.

What are Familiar Spirits?

Familiar spirits are demonic beings who will give details about a beloved member of the family who has died. We are expressly forbidden, of course, from seeking after the familiar spirits used in spiritualism. We are also forbidden to ask them questions about the future, etc., as the spiritualist would do.

> "Give no regard to mediums and familiar spirits; do not seek after them, to be defiled by them: I am the Lord your God."
>
> (Leviticus 19:31)

Isaiah confirms this word and asserts that it is a vain and foolish thing to do:

"And when they say to you, 'Seek those who are mediums and wizards, who whisper and mutter,' should not a people seek their God? Should they seek the dead on behalf of the living?" (Isaiah 8:19)

We are therefore expressly forbidden in Scripture to have anything to do with mediums, or familiar spirits, but sometimes they will attach themselves to a curse which has been put against a family, or to a sin which has been committed. There are a number of ways in which they may obtain an entrance to a family, one of which is through generational sin. They will latch onto the weakness that may have been sown into the family line, and they will seek to seal that weakness in, in order to stay within the familiar setting. They will seek to transfer from one member of the family to another at the moment of death.

The familiar spirit will thus continue down the family line and will actively encourage the weakness, the flaw and the perversity to persist within the generations. Thus the family is not only fighting against the weakness or the tendency to sin in a particular area, but it is also contesting against the familiar spirit. Of course, if a member of the family specifically sins by consulting a medium or a familiar spirit, then that would be an open invitation for that familiar spirit to enter the family line and take up residence.

It is very enlightening to see that King Saul consulted a familiar spirit in order to bring Samuel the prophet back from the dead, and also that King Manasseh, that very wicked king of Judah,

" . . . made his son pass through the fire, practised soothsaying, used witchcraft, and consulted spiritists and mediums. He did much evil in the sight of the Lord, to provoke Him to anger." (2 Kings 21:6)

As a general rule, when we are ministering into this area of generational iniquity, it is very important to check out whether there are any demonic familiar spirits present, and if so, we need to bind them and cast them out. The person you are praying with will also need to repent on behalf of their ancestors for inviting or allowing them in, and they will need to renounce the work of the enemy as well. We will be considering the subject of how we can be set free from generational iniquity in more depth in a later chapter.

First of all we need to understand how we can discover what damage has been introduced into our family line, and therefore what weaknesses, flaws, tendencies or curses are at work there.

Chapter 10
Discovering Your Family Weaknesses

Before we can receive freedom from generational iniquity we need to know what is at work within **our own** family line, in order that we may take accountability for it and thus bring it before God in confession and repentance. Therefore the question is: "How can we know what are the sins of our ancestors?" It is very important to realise that some of us will know very little about our family line, especially if we were orphaned or adopted at birth. Maybe, as in the story of one lady, the family had never been a close one and the relatives were kept very much at a distance. In such instances, we can have confidence in the mercy of God, and in a general way confess the sins of our ancestors believing and trusting Him for our cleansing and deliverance.

For those people who do know something about their family background, there are a number of avenues that can be explored. For example, we can look at and **observe** our parents, our grandparents, and even our great-grandparents, to see what is at work within their lives; that is, if such knowledge is available to us. We can **enquire** of those who know something about our family history; it may be that other relatives and friends of the family will be a mine of information. Much can be gleaned from them without entering into any unnecessary gossip.

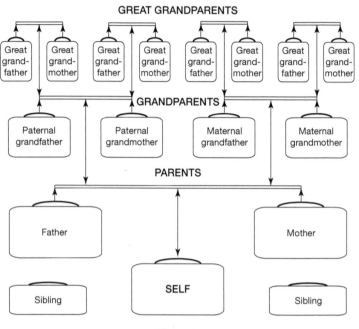

FAMILY LUGGAGE/BAGGAGE

Figure 1

Another method is to use a "**Family Luggage/Baggage**" sheet (Figure 1), which will help you to see pictorially at a glance the repeating of the patterns, which may be travelling down the family line.

We have already looked at some of these in a previous chapter. but another one, which you may notice, is the pattern of grandmother, mother and daughter, who all dominate and despise their husbands. Ezekiel 16:44–45 is very much up to date:

> *"You are your mother's daughter, loathing husband and children; and you are the sister of your sisters, who loathed their husbands and children."*

Other patterns, which may become evident, are the various addictive behaviours: alcoholism, drug abuse and adultery being fairly common.

You may also be aware that in your family there is a dabbling in, or a drawing towards false religions: Spiritualism, Freemasonry, or the New Age. In this area it may also be noticeable that confusion, sleepiness, and an enticement towards occultic practices is also apparent, especially when you try to concentrate in worship, read the scriptures or try to pray.

Sometimes it will be seen that there are frequent infirmities travelling down the family line, such illnesses as cancer, abortions, early death, miscarriages, and childlessness to name but a few. We have already seen that this may be as a result of a curse. One lady was convinced that she was the first person in her family ever to have an abortion. To her great surprise, when she shared the truth about the abortion with her mother, she was informed that a number of other women in the family had also had abortions, but everyone had been sworn to secrecy. They remembered that in the history of the family there was often talk concerning a "gypsy curse".

Painful emotions can also travel down the family line and these are often linked with the original sin. There may be rejection or a fear of rejection in the family, as happened to one young girl I prayed for. She asked for help because her peers were constantly rejecting her. On inquiring about her family history, she told me that her father had been put out of the house by his grandfather and not allowed to see his family again for many years, because of something which he had done. The father had never forgiven his grandfather and constantly feared more rejection. The fear of rejection had passed down the line from father to daughter and she had inherited and reaped the consequences of further rejection.

One man came to us for prayer because of the deep rage, which would often well up within him, in response to a situation, which was unjust. The rage was totally out of keeping with the circumstances he was facing at the time. On spending some time with him we all were surprised to discover that his grandfather had been involved in a drunken row and in a blind and furious rage had killed a neighbour. That original murder had brought into the family line a tendency towards violence and anger: the sins of the fathers visited upon the children to the third and fourth generation. His father had also suffered violent outbreaks of anger at, and on, inappropriate occasions.

The following are some of the possible sins or weaknesses, which I have personally ministered into on a regular basis and that, are, to some extent fairly common. Fears, phobias, depression, death, grief, disappointment, guilt, false guilt, shame, anxiety, and suicide can all be introduced into the generations either through a particular sin or through a curse and they will continue to have repercussions within the family if they are not dealt with. We have already seen that sexual sin or any kind of abuse (verbal, emotional, physical, and sexual), or sexual perversion, may all be observed to be at work within the family.

Once we have discerned what is at work and where our family weaknesses lie, then we can begin to deal with them, for the good news is that God has already provided the way of escape through the work of the Lord Jesus Christ upon the Cross.

Chapter 11

The Power of the Cross

How do we get free from the generational iniquity within our family line? Thank God that He has already provided a way of escape for us, for Jesus Christ bears our iniquities on the Cross, as well as our sins. In other words He carries the punishment for our own personal sins, as well as the consequences of our ancestor's sin. The Cross is God's answer to the intricate problem of man's sin, his sicknesses, his brokenness, his curses, his griefs, his sorrows, as well as the iniquity which he carries from his ancestors. According to the prophet Isaiah, our iniquity has been borne by Jesus on the Cross:

> *"But He was wounded for our transgressions,*
> *He was bruised for our iniquities;*
> *The chastisement for our peace was upon Him,*
> *And by His stripes we are healed.*
> *All we like sheep have gone astray;*
> *We have turned, every one, to his own way;*
> *And the Lord has laid on Him the iniquity of us all."*
>
> (Isaiah 53:5–6)

Isn't that a tremendous word of encouragement? There is no condition of man which is not covered by the work of the Lord Jesus Christ upon the Cross.

There is a very interesting picture of the work of Jesus on the Cross, graphically told in Scripture in the book of Leviticus chapter 16, which depicts certain aspects of the atonement. This is the picture of the two goats which were to be presented before God, one of which would be killed and its blood shed for the sins of the people of Israel. It would be a sin offering used for the cleansing of the people; this was to be known as the **sacrificed goat**.

> *"Then he shall kill the goat of the sin offering, which is for the people, bring its blood inside the veil, do with that blood as he did with the blood of the bull, and sprinkle it on the mercy seat and before the mercy seat. So he shall make atonement for the Holy Place, because of the uncleanness of the children of Israel, and because of their transgressions, for all their sins."* (Leviticus 16:15–16)

In Leviticus 16:21–22 we read of the purpose of the second goat, the life of which was to be retained, but burdened and separated to bear Israel's iniquity. This goat was to be known as the **scapegoat**.

> *"And Aaron shall lay both his hands on the head of the live goat, confess over it all the iniquities of the children of Israel, and all their transgressions, concerning all their sins, putting them on the head of the goat, and shall send it away into the wilderness by the hand of a suitable man. The goat shall bear on itself all their iniquities to an uninhabited land."* (Leviticus 16:21–22)

The picture of the two goats gives us a very vivid description of the work of Jesus upon the Cross, for His work is the fulfilment of both the sacrificed goat and the scapegoat. The Cross deals with both the punishment and the consequences of our own sin, and also it is at the Cross where we can be set free from the evil effects of the sins and the iniquities of our ancestors.

Two very important questions would seem to be:

- "How do we apply the work of Jesus on the Cross to our family sin?"
- "How can we be released from the sins, the flaw, the weakness and the tendency to sin in our family line and make-up which we have inherited from our ancestors?"

Scripture, fortunately gives us the answer. It is that we find release in the same way in which we found it when we entered into freedom from **our own** personal sin.

First, we need to **recognise** what the iniquities are, and after we do so, we need to take a **responsibility and an account- ability** for them as a member of the family line. We then need to stand up and be counted and **confess** and **repent** for the sins of our family, on **behalf** of the family. There is a scriptural precedent for doing this and the promise is that God will hear our **confession and repentance of ancestral sin**:

> *"But if they confess their iniquity and the iniquity of their fathers, with their unfaithfulness in which they were unfaithful to Me, and that they also have walked contrary to Me . . . Then I will remember My covenant."* (Leviticus 26:40, 42)

Nehemiah repented on behalf of his family line; he recog- nised and took responsibility for the sin of corruption and the breaking of God's commandments, and he confessed and repented for them before God. Nehemiah chapter 1 records his confession and repentance, not for his own sin, but for the sin of his family and his nation.

"We have acted very corruptly against You, and have not kept the commandments, the statues, nor the ordinances which You commanded Your servant Moses." (Nehemiah 1:7)

The leadership of Israel also took responsibility for the nation's generational sin:

"Then those of Israelite lineage separated themselves from all foreigners; and they stood and confessed their sins and the iniquities of their fathers." (Nehemiah 9:2)

Ezra also confessed and repented on behalf of his ancestors. We read that he repented of the sin of taking foreign wives and of taking on board their abominations, their idols and false worship. It is very interesting to note that, in actuality, Ezra had not committed these sins personally. He had not taken a foreign wife or worshipped any idols but he was identifying himself with his family's sin, and thus repenting on behalf of his nation and his generational line.

"At the evening sacrifice I arose from my fasting; and having torn my garment and my robe, I fell on my knees and spread out my hands to the Lord my God, and said, 'Oh my God: I am too ashamed and humiliated to lift up my face to You, my God; for our iniquities have risen higher than our heads, and our guilt has grown up to the heavens. Since the day of our fathers to this day we have been guilty.'"
(Ezra 9:5–6)

That is a lovely example of confession and repentance.

As we have seen with the prayer of Ezra and Nehemiah, there is a place for taking accountability for the sins of the ancestors. Just as we personally need to take accountability and responsibility for our own sin, so in the area of generational sin, there comes a time when some member of the family needs to take responsibility for the family sin.

Will God forgive? Will He remove our iniquity from us? Will He deliver us from the weakness, and the flaw in our family line? For encouragement in this, let me refer you to the story of Joshua the high priest.

> *"Then he showed me Joshua the high priest standing before the Angel of the Lord, and Satan standing at his right hand to oppose him."*
> (Zechariah 3:1)

The Lord speaks to Satan and rebukes him for his opposition to Joshua, who is evidently clothed in dirty and unkempt garments.

> *"Now Joshua was clothed with filthy garments, and was standing before the Angel. Then He answered and spoke to those who stood before Him, saying, 'Take away the filthy garments from him.' And to him He said, 'See, I have removed your iniquity from you, and I will clothe you with rich robes.'"* (Zechariah 3:3–4)

God will forgive. He has provided a way through Jesus to remove our dirty clothes of iniquity from us and He will dress us in His robe of righteousness. In Isaiah chapter 61, we have that lovely encouragement:

> *"I will greatly rejoice in the Lord,*
> *My soul shall be joyful in my God;*
> *For He has clothed me with the garments of salvation,*
> *He has covered me with the robe of righteousness,*
> *As a bridegroom decks himself with ornaments,*
> *And as a bride adorns herself with jewels."* (Isaiah 61:10)

So God has promised to set us free from our sins and our iniquities, and as we close the door on our old sinful family line, with all of its weaknesses, so we can ask the Holy Spirit to seal that door with the precious blood of Jesus.

The Good News, however, doesn't end there, for something vital and dynamic was being made available to us through the work of the Lord Jesus Christ upon the Cross; for the work of the Cross is both negative and positive. The negative being that He removes our sin and our generational iniquity from us; through confession and repentance, the door is finally closed and sealed. The positive being that at the Cross we walk through a new door; a door of blessing, a door of new beginnings. For it is at the Cross that Jesus welcomes us into a new family, His family – the **family of God**.

When we are "born again" through the work of the Holy Spirit, we become part of His family, we become **children of God**, and we inherit all the **blessings** which are His, and which He has won for us through the Cross. He is the second Adam, and as such, His family line is pure and without blemish. He gives to us His robe of righteousness.

The Will of God

On the subject of becoming part of a new family through the Cross, it is vital for us to understand that a mighty work of grace was actually taking place within the confines of the Garden of Gethsemane prior to Jesus' death. Jesus needed to deal with the sin and the stubbornness of the will of mankind. On the night in which Jesus was betrayed, we see Jesus bending the "will of man" towards the "will of God". Three times He cries out to God:

*"Abba, Father, all things are possible for You. Take this cup away from me; nevertheless, **not what I will, but what You will.**"*

(Mark 14:36)

It was in another garden, the Garden of Eden, where the first Adam allowed his will, which originally was bent toward the will of God, to be twisted and bent toward the will of Satan. It was thus in the Garden of Gethsemane that Jesus, at a great cost known only to Himself, bent the "will of man" back again towards "the will of God". With great drops of blood and through enormous stress and distress, He began a new family line which was based on His obedience to the Father, and as we have seen from Deuteronomy chapter 28, obedience brings blessing.

Of course, if that was all that there was available in the Cross it would be wonderful, but we would no doubt, still struggle to obey God's laws ourselves. We understand that Jesus' will was bent towards the will of God, but what about ours? The Scriptures tell us that even that is taken care of. For not only are we "adopted", "transferred" into a new family line, we are also given the "**family disposition**", so that we too can live obedient and blessed lives which will flow through us to our children and to "our children's children".

According to Jeremiah the prophet, God says:

"I will put My law in their minds, and write it on their hearts; and I will be their God, and they shall be My people . . . I will forgive their iniquity, and their sin I will remember no more."

(Jeremiah 31:33, 34)

The original laws of God were written on stone, but now they are to be written within – on our minds and on our hearts. Thus we will be enabled to "know" the law of God in our thinking and be able to "obey" the law from the most innermost part of our being – even our hearts. However, not only are we given the "family disposition" we are also given the **"family Spirit"** – the Holy Spirit. The tremendous fact is that God has given to us another promise, a promise that He will put His own Spirit within us, which will enable us and empower us to fulfil His laws from a glad heart.

> *"I will put My Spirit within you and cause you to walk in My statues, and you will keep My judgements and do them."* (Ezekiel 36:27)

Thus we begin to live under the New Covenant, the covenant of blessing through obedience, which is made available to us through the work of the Lord Jesus Christ. The plans and purposes of God will thus be fulfilled, in that He will have a people of His own, who are part of His family, filled with His Spirit, and obedient to His laws. The cry of their hearts will be the same as the cry of Jesus, the Head of the family:

> *"I do not seek My own will but the will of the Father who sent Me."*
> (John 5:30)

Thus the **law of blessing**, the **law of multiplication** and the **law of sowing and reaping** will be restored to their original purposes, for the desire of God's heart is to always be:

> *" . . . showing mercy to thousands, to those who love Me and keep My commandments."* (Exodus 20:6)

Appendix

Suggested Prayer of Release from Generational Iniquity

A prayer, confessing the sins of the family and breaking the links:

"Father, I thank You that on the Cross You have dealt with all of my sin, through the death and resurrection of the Lord Jesus Christ. Thank You that He paid the penalty for my sins through His shed blood, and that He also carried the punishment for the sins and the iniquities of my ancestors. I thank You too, that according to Your Word, I can come and confess the sins of my forefathers. I do gladly and humbly repent of the sins which my family line have committed back to the third and fourth generation, and to the tenth generation for sexual sin. I especially repent of _____ [*speak out any specific sins, which you know your family has been into; sexual, addictive, etc.*].

I also repent of any false worship, which they have given _____ [*speak out any that are relevant, e.g. Freemasonry, Spiritualism, Buddhism, etc.*].

I also repent of any occultic activity in my family line _____ [*speak out any that is known; tarot cards, horoscopes, etc.*].

Father God, I confess these sins and weaknesses, which may have affected me, and I freely forgive my ancestors in Jesus' Name. I repent and turn away from my own sins in these areas and I renounce Satan and all of his works. I ask You, Heavenly Father, to forgive our sin and to set me, and my family line, free from the consequences of generational iniquity. I ask that the door may be closed and sealed with the precious blood of Jesus. In His Name I pray. Amen."

Generational and
Family Blessings

Contents

Preface

A number of years ago I wrote a small book entitled *Freedom from Generational Sin*. This looked at the subject of the possible consequences of sin committed by an ancestor travelling down the family line to affect the present and future generations. The book also included how to be set free from the consequences of such sin.

Since writing that book I have also taught the opposite scriptural viewpoint that it was God's original intention for blessing to flow down a godly family line – through those who are seeking to be obedient to His will. I would like to emphasise that in this book we are looking at spiritual rather than material blessings.

Having taught this subject on a number of occasions I have been asked if the teaching is in print, hence this book. I pray that it will be a blessing and an encouragement to you that God's heart is to bless you and your children and your children's children.

Ruth Hawkey

Chapter 1

The Father's Heart Is to Bless

The words "bless" or "blessing" occur four hundred and ten times in the Scriptures. This highlights the importance of the subject and shows us that it is in the heart of God, Creator of this world, to pour blessings upon all of His creation.

As we shall see in a later chapter the Scriptures also teach us that our Heavenly Father desires to pour blessings upon His children: those who trust in Him and have been born into His family through His Son Jesus Christ.

> " . . . *showing mercy to thousands, to those who love Me and keep My commandments.*" (Exodus 20:6)

Truly it is God's heart to bless His world and His people. Let us briefly remind ourselves of the many ways in which God does this.

The Father's Heart Is to Bless His Creation

God spoke His world into being and then proceeded to bless that which He had created: He blessed the animals; the sea creatures; the birds; the sun, moon and stars; the rivers and waterfalls; the hills and mountains; the flowers and trees; all of His creation rests in the blessing of His continuing mercy and care. According to Lamentations 3:23 we are assured that God's compassion and mercy never fails:

> *"They are new every morning;*
> *Great is Your faithfulness."*

We are also told in Genesis 1:21–22 that:

> *"God created great sea creatures and every living thing that moves, with which the waters abounded, according to their kind, and every winged bird according to its kind. And God saw that it was good. And God blessed them . . . "*

How exciting it is to remember, when we look around at our world, that it is a place which is under God's blessing.

We are also reminded in Genesis 1:27–28 that God also created and blessed mankind:

> *"So God created man in His own image; in the image of God He created him; male and female He created them. Then God blessed them . . . "*

From the Scriptures we can also see that it is God's heart to multiply all of these blessings down through the generational line to all of His people:

> *"And God blessed them, saying, 'Be fruitful and multiply, and fill the waters in the seas . . . '"*   (Genesis 1:22)

The Blessing of God Is Shown by the Variety of His Creation

When we look at the world which God has created we are also reminded of the fact that God our Father loves variety and individuality. His blessing rests upon a wealth of multiplicity. We only have to look at the colour, the beauty and the diversity of nature, the appeal to the senses of the different seasons and the uniqueness of people and variety of cultures to realise what an amazing Creator our Father God is. Trees, animals, flowers, birds, people, fish and flowers all speak of a God who loves our individuality and wants to bless it. To realise that you are unique and priceless – one who is made in God's image – is a deep truth to be treasured.

The Blessing of the Father's Sustaining Grace

As well as God enjoying variety and blessing our uniqueness, it is also important to remember that it is God who blesses us by keeping the stars in place; whose command keeps the sea within its allocated boundaries; whose laws of the universe continue year after year and whose love is new every morning. God "spoke" the world into being and the world, as we know it, could just as easily be "unspoken". In fact, we rely on the very nature of God for the sustaining and continuance of His creation.

The Blessing of Being Able to Rely on the Very Nature of God

We are told in the Scriptures that **God's Name** and all which that entails continues throughout all generations:

> *"Your name, O LORD, endures forever,*
> *Your fame, O LORD, throughout all generations."* (Psalm 135:13)

When Moses asked God what he should call Him, God answered:

> *"'I AM WHO I AM.' And He said, 'Thus you shall say to the children of Israel, "I AM has sent me to you."'"* (Exodus 3:14)

In other words God's name is eternal and we can rest on the fact that He never changes.

We are also encouraged to rely on the truth that because of **God's mercy** we are not consumed:

> *"Through the Lord's mercies we are not consumed,*
> *Because His compassions fail not.*
> *They are new every morning . . . "* (Lamentations 3:22–23)

Thus we are blessed by the knowledge that God's **mercy** is new every morning and, as the psalmist reiterates, His mercy is also eternal:

> *"For the Lord is good;*
> *His mercy is everlasting,*
> *And His truth endures to all generations."* (Psalm 100:5)

According to the Scriptures we can also trust in the **faithfulness of God**:

> *"Your faithfulness endures to all generations . . . "* (Psalm 119:90)

Without God's faithfulness, mercy and sustaining grace the world as we know it would cease to exist.

The Blessing of the Sabbath Day

As well as blessing creation God has also placed a special blessing upon the Sabbath day:

"Then God blessed the seventh day and sanctified it, because in it He rested from all His work which God had created and made."

(Genesis 2:3)

This reminds us of the importance of having times of rest in the midst of our busy work schedules. Our Heavenly Father knows that as His children we can only sustain a certain amount of work pressure and we do well to heed His provision of the "Sabbath rest" which is meant to be a blessing and not an unnecessary interruption of the working week.

The Laws of the Universe

We need to recognise, however, that there are **certain laws linked into the Father's blessing**. Because we live in a world of cause and effect God has written certain conditions into His universe which are linked to God's ability to bless His people. For example, there is the **law of sowing and reaping**. We are told that:

" . . . whatever a man sows, that he will also reap."

(Galatians 6:7)

God can only bless us when we sow good and honourable things into our lives.

The **law of faith** is also linked to God's blessing as Jesus demonstrated:

"Then He touched their eyes, saying, 'According to your faith let it be to you.' " (Matthew 9:29)

We need to exercise our faith in a faithful God and to live in the knowledge that it is His heart to bless us.

Related to the law of blessing is the **law of obedience**. One of the conditions of God being able to bless us is that we are obedient to His commandments. We see the promise of this in Deuteronomy 28:1–2:

> *"Now it shall come to pass, if you diligently obey the voice of the LORD your God, to observe carefully all His commandments which I command you today, that the LORD your God will set you high above all nations of the earth. And all these blessings shall come upon you and overtake you, because you obey the voice of the LORD your God."*

Chapter 2

Household Blessing

We have an abundant God; a generous Heavenly Father, whose heart is to bless His creation and especially His children as they walk according to His laws. Whilst God is committed to blessing the individual who bases his life upon God's Word and who lives according to His commandments, we shall see from the Scriptures that He also desires to bless our families.

We can see many examples of this in the Old Testament. For example, God's promise to Abraham was a promise of blessing not only to Abraham but also to Sarah and their future family:

"And I will bless her and also give you a son by her; then I will bless her, and she shall be a mother of nations; kings of peoples shall be from her." (Genesis 17:16)

And in Genesis 22:17 God talks again about His multiplication of blessings to Abraham and his family:

"blessing I will bless you, and multiplying I will multiply your descendants as the stars of the heaven and as the sand which is on the seashore; and your descendants shall possess the gate of their enemies."

Another family which God chose to bless was the family of

Noah, who was blessed by being saved from destruction through the flood:

> *"Then the Lord said to Noah, 'Come into the ark, **you and all your household**, because I have seen that you are righteous before Me in this generation.'"* (Genesis 7:1, emphasis added)

Noah was a good man and we are told that his righteousness had wonderful consequences for his whole family. The ark was not just for Noah, it was for his household. The Bible says that Noah was righteous but it says nothing about the righteousness of his family – nevertheless they were all saved. This encourages us to believe that a new believer can bring all of his family into the ark, into that position of safety. They are all meant to be partakers of God's blessing. We are told in the book of James that:

> *"The effective, fervent prayer of a righteous man avails much."* (James 5:16)

This suggests that God's blessing is enabled to flow to our families when we are walking according to God's laws; when we are seeking to be righteous and when we are spending time in prayer on their behalf.

Job was a man who knew the blessing of being protected by God – a fact which grieved Satan so much that he confronted God about Job's position:

> *"So Satan answered the Lord and said, 'Does Job fear God for nothing? **Have You not made a hedge around him, around his household, and around all that he has on every side?**'"* (Job 1:9–10, emphasis added)

Will you note that, even by Satan's own admission, Job's family had a hedge of protection around them? The Scriptures tell us that this was because Job was a righteous man who feared God:

> *"Then the L*ORD *said to Satan, 'Have you considered My servant Job, that there is none like him on the earth, a blameless and upright man, one who fears God and shuns evil?' So Satan answered the L*ORD *and said, 'Does Job fear God for nothing?'"* (Job 1:8–9)

Satan then goes on to tempt Job away from faith and obedience so that the blessing of the hedge of protection could be taken away.

Another family in the Old Testament who was blessed by God was the family of a man called Obed-Edom. He was a Philistine in whose house the Ark of the Covenant rested for three months and because of this God blessed Obed-Edom's family:

> *"The ark of the L*ORD *remained in the house of Obed-Edom the Gittite three months. **And the Lord blessed Obed-Edom and all his household.**"* (2 Samuel 6:11, emphasis added)

The New Testament

When we look at the New Testament we see that the same pattern is repeated. It also confirms the principle that God desires to bless not only individuals, but also their families. For example, in John's Gospel chapter 4, we have the story of the nobleman whose son was sick. Not only was the son healed but the nobleman's whole family were saved:

> *"And there was a certain nobleman whose son was sick at Capernaum. When he heard that Jesus had come out of Judea into Galilee, he went*

to Him and implored Him to come down and heal his son, for he was
at the point of death. "   (John 4:46–47)

The story continues in verse 50:

"Jesus said to him, 'Go your way; your son lives.' So the man believed
the word that Jesus spoke to him, and he went his way. And as he
was now going down, his servants met him and told him, saying,
'Your son lives!' Then he inquired of them the hour when he
got better. And they said to him, 'Yesterday at the seventh hour
the fever left him.' So the father knew that it was at the same
hour in which Jesus said to him, 'Your son lives.' **And he himself**
believed, and his whole household. "

(John 4:50–53, emphasis added)

Only the son was healed but the nobleman and the whole
household trusted in the Lord. Thus although only the son
received the grace of healing, nevertheless all of the family
turned to the Lord. This also tells us something about the place
of healing in evangelism.

We see the same principle at work in the family of Cornelius
when he desired the filling of the Holy Spirit. We are told that
he was:

"a devout man and one who feared God with all his household, who
gave alms generously to the people, and prayed to God always."

(Acts 10:2)

Cornelius was encouraged to send for Peter the Apostle:

"who will tell you words **by which you and all your household will**
be saved. "   (Acts 11:14, emphasis added)

So Cornelius invited his relatives, friends and family to hear Peter and it was as Peter spoke that the Holy Spirit fell upon them and all that were in the house were saved.

We see the same attitude being repeated in the family of Lydia who was baptized along with her whole household:

> *"And when **she and her household were baptized**, she begged us, saying, 'If you have judged me to be faithful to the Lord, come to my house and stay.' So she persuaded us."*
>
> (Acts 16:15, emphasis added)

When the Philippian jailor believed we are told that his family were promised salvation as well:

> *"So they said, 'Believe on the Lord Jesus Christ, and **you will be saved, you and your household.'"***   (Acts 16:31, emphasis added)

Was the promise to the jailor fulfilled? Yes it was:

> *"Now when he had brought them into his house, he set food before them; and he rejoiced, having **believed in God with all his household**."*
>
> (Acts 16:34, emphasis added)

All of Stephanas' family were saved and baptized:

> *"Yes, I also **baptized the household of Stephanas**."*
>
> (1 Corinthians 1:16, emphasis added)

As was the family of Crispus:

> *"Then Crispus, the ruler of the synagogue, **believed on the Lord with all his household**."*   (Acts 18:8, emphasis added)

Believing by the household in those days far exceeded what we see today. Paul prayed that the whole family of Onesiphorus would be shown mercy – not just Onesiphorus himself:

> *"Greet Prisca and Aquila, and the household of Onesiphorus."*
>
> (2 Timothy 4:19)

> **"The Lord grant mercy to the household of Onesiphorus,** *for he often refreshed me, and was not ashamed of my chain."*
>
> (2 Timothy 1:16, emphasis added)

Thus we see that according to the Old and New Testaments it is God's heart to bless not only the individual but also their family. It could also be argued that if they had servants, which some of them had, then the servants were included in the blessing of salvation. This does not of course take away from the fact or necessity of individual repentance and conversion but rather shows what we can confidently come to God and ask Him for our children's salvation. The words are true: *"You have not because you ask not."* If we know that "family salvation" is on the heart of God then we can ask more confidently being assured that it is in accordance with His will.

Chapter 3
Generational Blessing

According to the Scriptures God's blessing is meant to go even further that that of blessing our own personal family. God's heart is to pour His blessings down our family line to our future generations. When God's people obey God's commandments and walk in faith and obedience to them then the blessings which God confers on them are passed down the generational line and, we are told, multiplied for a thousand generations:

> *"Oh, that they had such a heart in them that they would fear Me and always keep all My commandments, that it might be well with them and with their children forever!"* (Deuteronomy 5:29)

> *"The righteous man walks in his integrity.*
> *His children are blessed after him."* (Proverbs 20:7)

Scripture tells us that the blessing of faith can travel down the family line and gives us the example of Timothy's inheritance of faith from his grandmother and mother:

> *"I call to remembrance the genuine faith that is in you, which was also in your grandmother Lois and your mother Eunice . . . "*
> (2 Timothy 1:5)

We are not told whether it was Timothy's grandmother on his father or his mother's side; one assumes the mother since the father is not mentioned.

We are also encouraged to believe that mercy travels down the family line, yes even the mercy of God to those who love and honour Him:

> *"Therefore know that the LORD your God, He is God, the faithful*
> *God who keeps covenant and mercy for a thousand generations with*
> *those who love Him and keep His commandments."*
>
> (Deuteronomy 7:9)

And, of course, we can be assured, according to the Scriptures, of God's righteousness being available for our grandchildren:

> *"The mercy of the LORD is from everlasting to everlasting*
> *On those who fear Him,*
> *And His righteousness to children's children."*   (Psalm 103:17)

We see the evidence of God's blessing upon the generational line when we consider the family of Adam. When Adam sinned he forfeited his position in the Garden of Eden where he used to walk and talk with God on a regular basis. However, we can see the tremendous mercy and blessing of God upon Adam's future generational line in that one of Adam's descendants, Enoch, like Adam, also walked with God. What a blessing for Adam and Eve:

> *"After he begot Methuselah, Enoch walked with God three hundred*
> *years, and had sons and daughters. So all the days of Enoch were three*
> *hundred and sixty-five years. And Enoch walked with God; and he*
> *was not, for God took him."*   (Genesis 5:22–24)

According to a literal interpretation of Genesis 5, the abundance of God's blessing can also be seen in the fact that God actually allowed Adam to live to see this happening as shown in Figure 1.

Figure 1: Adam's Family Line According to Genesis 5
Adam was 130 when Seth was born (v. 3) and Adam died when he was 930 (v. 5). The following table shows Adam's age when his descendants were born:

Adam's age	Descendants
235	Seth was 105 when Enosh was born (v. 6) and died when he was 912 (v. 8).
325	Enosh was 90 when Cainan was born (v. 9) and died when he was 905 (v. 11).
395	Cainan was 70 when Mahalalel was born (v. 12) and died when he was 910 (v. 14).
460	Mahalalel was 65 when Jared was born (v. 15) and died when he was 895 (v. 17).
622	Jared was 162 when Enoch was born (v. 18) and died when he was 962 (v. 20).
687	**Enoch was 65 when Methuselah was born (v. 21) but did not die for God took him when he was 365 (v. 23).**
	Methuselah was 187 when Lamech was born (v. 25) and died when he was 969 (v. 27).
	Lamech was 182 when Noah was born (v. 28) and died when he was 777 (v. 31)

Adam, if he had lived, would have been one thousand and fifty-six years old by the time Noah the son of Lamech was born, but, as we have seen, Adam died when he was nine hundred and thirty years old. Just to complete the picture Noah was over five hundred years old when Shem, Ham and Japheth were born

(v. 32) and Noah died when he was nine hundred and fifty years old (Genesis 9:29).

Thus a literal interpretation would suggest that Adam was still alive (six hundred and twenty-two years old) when Enoch was born! However, according to the *New Bible Dictionary*: "genealogies, including those of Genesis 5 . . . must always be used with great restraint whenever it appears that they are open to more than one interpretation".[1] The interesting point is that even though Adam sinned he still had a descendant who "walked with God" as he had! What a blessing – truly a merciful God.

Generational Blessing in Abraham's Family

As well as the family line of Adam and Eve there are many other instances of generational blessing within the Scriptures, of which perhaps the most well known is that of Abraham. God's plan to bless Abraham always included his future descendants – the Jewish people. God declared that through Isaac Abraham's descendants were going to be as numerous as the stars and that:

> " . . . *all the nations of the earth shall be blessed, because you have obeyed My voice.*"
> (Genesis 22:18)

The promised blessing was stated again to Abraham's son Isaac:

> "*I will make your descendants multiply as the stars of heaven; I will give to your descendants all these lands; and in your seed all the nations of the earth shall be blessed.*"
> (Genesis 26:4)

There came a day when God reiterates the promised blessing to Abraham's grandson Jacob. God promises him that:

" . . . the land on which you lie I will give to you and your descendants. Also your descendants shall be as the dust of the earth; you shall spread abroad to the west and the east, to the north and the south; and in you and in your seed all the families of the earth shall be blessed."

(Genesis 28:13–14)

We don't have to look far in the Scriptures to see that the promised blessing is also there with Abraham's great grandson Joseph:

"The LORD was with Joseph, and he was a successful man; and he was in the house of his master the Egyptian . . . and the blessing of the LORD was on all that he had in the house and in the field."

(Genesis 39:2, 5)

The blessing is also pronounced on Abraham's other great grandson, Judah:

"The sceptre shall not depart from Judah,
Nor a lawgiver from between his feet,
Until Shiloh comes."　　　　　　　　　　(Genesis 49:10)

This blessing continues down the family line to King David – who was of the family of Judah and will indeed continue into eternity.

"And your house and your kingdom shall be established forever before you. Your throne shall be established forever."　　(2 Samuel 7:16)

In 2 Samuel 2:4 we read:

"Then the men of Judah came, and there they anointed David king over the house of Judah."

97

The blessing carries on down the generational line to Solomon and his descendants, for King David is promised that his son Solomon will know the blessing of God and that God will be his Father:

> " . . . and I will establish the throne of his kingdom over Israel forever."   (1 Chronicles 22:10)

And of course God's promised blessings also included Jesus who was of the line of Judah:

> "From this man's seed [David], according to the promise, God raised up for Israel a Saviour – Jesus."   (Acts 13:23)

God's Blessing to Descendants of Obed-Edom

We have already considered the blessing upon the household of Obed-Edom. However, the blessing didn't just rest upon him but was also evident on his sons and grandsons. They were described as men of great ability; *"able men with strength for work"*. Their history is recorded in 1 Chronicles 26:4–8:

> "Moreover the sons of Obed-Edom were Shemaiah the firstborn, Jehozabad the second, Joah the third, Sacar the fourth, Nethanel the fifth, Ammiel the sixth, Issachar the seventh, Peulthai the eighth; for God blessed him. Also to Shemaiah his son were sons born who governed their fathers' houses, because they were men of great ability. The sons of Shemaiah were Othni, Rephael, Obed, and Elzabad, whose brothers Elihu and Semachiah were able men. All these were of the sons of Obed-Edom, they and their sons and their brethren, able men with strength for the work: sixty-two of Obed-Edom."

More Old Testament Examples of Generational Blessing

Phinehas was another man whose generational line knew a great deal about the blessing of God. He was the son of Eleazar and the grandson of Aaron:

> *"Eleazar, Aaron's son, took for himself one of the daughters of Putiel as wife; and she bore him Phinehas."* (Exodus 6:25)

In Numbers 25:7–13 we have the story of Phinehas who saved the Israelites from the plague. An Israelite had sinned by marrying a foreign wife. Phinehas killed both the woman and the Israelite and thus turned away God's judgment from the nation. The Psalms also record this vital part of Israel's history:

> *"Then Phinehas stood up and intervened,*
> *And the plague was stopped.*
> *And that was accounted to him for righteousness*
> *To all generations forevermore."* (Psalm 106:30–31)

Ezra, who was a descendant of Aaron and Phinehas, also walked in his ancestors' blessing:

> *"Now after these things, in the reign of Artaxerxes king of Persia, Ezra the son of . . . Phinehas, the son of Eleazar, the son of Aaron the chief priest . . . the hand of the LORD his God upon him."*
> (Ezra 7:1, 5–6)

When we turn to the book of Ezra we can read the tremendous account of Ezra's contribution to Israel's history and there we see how God's blessing continued down his family line.

Caleb was a man who God promised to bless because he was

a man after God's own heart: a man of a different spirit. He was one of the two spies who brought back a good report, with Joshua, concerning the land of Canaan. He declared to Moses that he truly believed that God would give them the land. As we can see from the Scriptures, God, because of Caleb's faith, promised to bless his descendants as well.

> *"But My servant Caleb, because he has a different spirit in him and has followed Me fully, I will bring into the land where he went, and his descendants shall inherit it."* (Numbers 14:24)

Caleb's nephew was one of the descendants upon whom God bestowed His blessing: he turned out to be a very good judge in Israel:

> *"When the children of Israel cried out to the LORD, the LORD raised up a deliverer for the children of Israel, who delivered them: Othniel the son of Kenaz, Caleb's younger brother. The Spirit of the LORD came upon him, and he judged Israel."* (Judges 3:9–10)

It is interesting to note that in Caleb's line there was also a man called Nabal; he was the person who refused to help King David when he was in real need (1 Samuel 25). Nabal was very rich and prosperous but nevertheless he was also very stubborn and it was his wife Abigail who eventually helped David and became David's wife after Nabal died. (What was strength in Caleb – his determination – became a weakness in Nabal resulting in his stubbornness.)

Another generational line which was blessed by God was the family line of Rahab. In Joshua chapter 6 we read how Rahab took care of the two spies Joshua had sent into Jericho to look over the land, prior to Joshua's armies moving in to do battle.

She hid the spies on the roof of her house and was told to hang a scarlet thread out of the window of her house in order to remain safe. Everyone would be killed in Jericho except those within her house.

> *"So it shall be that whoever goes outside the doors of your house into the street, his blood shall be on his own head, and we will be guiltless. And whoever is with you in the house, his blood shall be on our head if a hand is laid on him."* (Joshua 2:19)

Rahab obeyed Joshua's instructions and she and all her household were saved when the walls of Jericho fell down. Rahab's future generational line is a very interesting one indeed, for she eventually married a man named Salmon:

> *"Salmon begot Boaz by Rahab, Boaz begot Obed by Ruth, Obed begot Jesse, and Jesse begot David the king. David the king begot Solomon by her who had been the wife of Uriah."* (Matthew 1:5–6)

Eventually, of course, the family line included Joseph the husband of Mary. This encourages us to believe that God can redeem and bless any family line that is willing to turn to Him and walk in His way.

According to the Scriptures other people can also be blessed because of God's righteous people: Jacob's uncle Laban asked Jacob to stay around because, as he says:

> *"I have learned by experience that the LORD has blessed me for your sake."* (Genesis 30:27)

Potiphar was another person who became aware that his family was being blessed because of someone else, in this case Joseph:

> *"So it was, from the time that he had made him overseer of his house . . . that the* LORD *blessed the Egyptian's house for Joseph's sake."*
>
> (Genesis 39:5)

This would seem to suggest that God's blessing has the potential of extending around a person to those within his work place or his extended family; in fact to any who come into contact with him in his wider sphere of influence.

Notes
1. *New Bible Dictionary*, Inter-Varsity Press, 1975, p. 213.

Chapter 4

Extent of God's Blessing

The question then arises as to what exactly do the Scriptures teach us concerning the extent of God's blessing upon the family and the future generational line? We will just consider one or two of the most obvious.

Salvation for the Family

According to Moses the Passover was something which was to be remembered and celebrated for the whole family. He writes that the Paschal lamb was for the household, not just for the individual:

> "Speak to all the congregation of Israel, saying: 'On the tenth day of this month every man shall take for himself a lamb, according to the house of his father, a lamb for a household.'" (Exodus 12:3)

Thus we see that the lamb was slain for the whole house and its blood put on the doorposts. Salvation was for the household:

> "And they shall take some of the blood and put it on the two doorposts and on the lintel of the houses where they eat it."
>
> (Exodus 12:7)

It reminds one of the household of Rahab where everyone who stayed in the house was saved. Thus we could argue that it is God's heart and intention to save families as well as individuals.

Peace to the Family

When Jesus sent His disciples out to the surrounding towns and villages to preach the Gospel, He gave them some very specific directions, which included speaking peace upon the family with whom they stayed – not just upon the individual:

> *"Now whatever city or town you enter, inquire who in it is worthy, and stay there till you go out. And when you go into a household, greet it. If the household is worthy, let your peace come upon it. But if it is not worthy, let your peace return to you."*
>
> (Matthew 10:11–13)

The Outpouring of the Holy Spirit upon the Generational Line

We are very aware that according to the sermon of Peter the Apostle, on the Day of Pentecost, the outpouring of the Holy Spirit was to be for the family as well as for the individual:

> *"For the promise is to you and to your children, and to all who are afar off, as many as the Lord our God will call."* (Acts 2:39)

It is especially important that heads of families take a hold of this promise and align their heart with God's heart, praying for their children to enter into the promise and experience of the Holy Spirit as well as themselves. Remember that His promise is to your children as well as to yourself.

We have been considering the fact that it is possible for spiritual blessings to travel down the family line but there are of course other blessings which it is possible to see repeated within the generational line; some of these could be described as Christian virtues whilst others are moral virtues. For example, in my family line there are at least five generations of Christians, which could be due to the faithfulness, the prayers and the righteousness of someone way back in my generational line. In other words no room for boasting or of a feeling of superiority!

I recently met a young woman in the Highlands of Scotland whose grandfather had waited on the quayside to pick up Duncan Campbell from the ferry when he visited the Isle of Lewis. It was through Duncan Campbell's ministry that a tremendous revival broke out. I soon discovered that this young girl had a great gift of prayer, a remarkable gift of intercession and a throbbing heartbeat for her native Scotland. Truly a blessing which had passed down from grandfather to granddaughter.

A gentleman who works in a Christian Ministry Centre shared with me recently that there have been members of his family, over many generations, who have been involved in missionary work in South Africa as well as in Rwanda – from his great, great, great grandparents up to the present day.

One of the Christian virtues present in abundance in our family line is that of joy and laughter. If my two sisters, my mother, my daughters and my grandchildren meet together I can guarantee that within two minutes there will be gales of laughter echoing throughout the house. In fact, we were at a niece's wedding just recently and one of the distant neighbours remarked that she could hear shouts of laughter from the top of the street!

On the other hand, someone might see that there are moral virtues such as courage, strength in adversity, kindness, dependability and loyalty repeatedly present in their family line. Others might see the blessings of creativity, music, the love of the outdoors, evident amongst their family members both present and past.

The Christian family is blessed, of course, because of the obedience of Jesus. According to Deuteronomy God says:

> *"I set before you today a blessing and a curse: the blessing, if you obey the commandments of the LORD your God which I command you today."* (Deuteronomy 11:26–27)

And the good news is that Jesus as Head of our family has:

> *" . . . humbled Himself and became obedient to the point of death."*
> (Philippians 2:8)

And therefore, because of His obedience, we have been blessed:

> *" . . . with every spiritual blessing in the heavenly places in Christ."*
> (Ephesians 1:3)

According to D.M. Lloyd-Jones in his book *God's Ultimate Purpose*[1] Paul is encouraging the Christians in Ephesus (and of course ourselves) to enter into the heritage won for us by Jesus and thus enjoy the Christian life as we should. He argues that before the world was created God drew up a great Covenant of Grace – God the Father said that He would grant forgiveness, reconciliation, restoration, new life and a new nature to all who belonged to His Son. The condition was that the Son would come into the world and bear the sin of mankind. Through His perfect obedience to the Father He was able to do this and thus, because of His obedience, we have the right to enter into the spiritual blessings which Jesus has won for us.

What are the spiritual blessings to which Paul is referring?

According to Francis Frangipane in his book *The Power of Covenant Prayer*[2] it is "everything we behold in the life of Jesus: the blessing of healing, and miracles, of virtue and deliverance."

The following are some of the many spiritual blessings which are part of the inheritance of those who belong to the Body of Christ. For example, we have the privilege of having been **chosen**:

> *"Blessed be the God and Father of our Lord Jesus Christ, who has blessed us with every spiritual blessing in the heavenly places in Christ, just as He chose us in Him before the foundation of the world."*
>
> (Ephesians 1:3–4)

We can know the blessing of **salvation** because of Jesus:

> *"For God so loved the world that He gave His only begotten Son, that whoever believes in Him should not perish but have everlasting life."*
>
> (John 3:16)

Another wonderful blessing is that of knowing the joy of **forgiveness**:

> *"If we confess our sins, He is faithful and just to forgive us our sins and to cleanse us from all unrighteousness."*   (1 John 1:9)

We also are blessed to know that 'in Christ' we are **new creations**:

> *"Therefore, if anyone is in Christ, he is a new creation; old things have passed away; behold, all things have become new."*
>
> (2 Corinthians 5:17)

Remember also that because of Jesus we have been **adopted** into God's family – what a blessing:

> *"For you did not receive the spirit of bondage again to fear, but you received the Spirit of adoption by whom we cry out, 'Abba, Father.' The Spirit Himself bears witness with our spirit that we are children of God, and if children, then heirs – heirs of God and joint heirs with Christ."*   (Romans 8:15–17)

We have also been wonderfully **justified** because of what Jesus accomplished for us upon the cross:

> *"Therefore let it be known to you, brethren, that through this Man is preached to you the forgiveness of sins; and by Him everyone who believes is justified from all things from which you could not be justified by the law of Moses."*   (Acts 13:38–39)

We can also know the amazing **peace** of Jesus within our hearts no matter what situations we are called upon to walk through:

> *"Therefore, having been justified by faith, we have peace with God through our Lord Jesus Christ, through whom also we have access by faith into this grace in which we stand."*   (Romans 5:1–2)

And of course we can continually know the blessing of being **filled with the Holy Spirit** and all that is included in that blessing:

> *"But you shall receive power when the Holy Spirit has come upon you."*   (Acts 1:8)

Therefore, we can know **His power, presence, gifts and fruit** – what a joy and what blessings are ours because of the obedience of Jesus. And joy of joys, blessing upon blessing, wonder upon wonders, because of Jesus we are also **glorified** in Him:

> *"Moreover whom He predestined, these He also called; whom He called, these He also justified; and whom He justified, these He also glorified."* (Romans 8:30)

Thus we have seen that it is God's heart is to bless His creation, individuals, families and future generations. However, as we have already noted there are certain conditions to be fulfilled in order for this to happen – faith and obedience seem to be key factors. It also appears to be necessary for a choice to be made by a person in authority within the household to follow God's commandments such as Joshua did when he challenged the Israelites:

> *"... choose for yourselves this day whom you will serve, whether the gods which your fathers served that were on the other side of the River, or the gods of the Amorites, in whose land you dwell. But as for me and my house, we will serve the Lord."* (Joshua 24:15)

Or as God testified about Abraham:

> *"For I have known him, in order that he may command his children and his household after him, that they keep the way of the Lord, to do righteousness and justice, that the Lord may bring to Abraham what He has spoken to him."* (Genesis 18:19)

Or as Jacob commanded his family:

> *"And Jacob said to his household and to all who were with him, 'Put away the foreign gods that are among you, purify yourselves, and change your garments.'"* (Genesis 35:2)

The "person in authority" would seem to be a husband, a wife or a single person who truly chooses to follow the Lord. According to Paul, writing to the Corinthians, he states that:

> *"The unbelieving husband is sanctified by the wife, and the unbelieving wife is sanctified by the husband; otherwise your children would be unclean, but now they are holy."*   (1 Corinthians 7:14)

When we consider the story of Lydia, who was a single business woman, it would appear that a single person has the same position of authority within the household:

> *"Now a certain woman named Lydia heard us. She was a seller of purple from the city of Thyatira, who worshipped God. The Lord opened her heart to heed the things spoken by Paul. And when she and her household were baptized, she begged us, saying, 'If you have judged me to be faithful to the Lord, come to my house and stay.'"*
> (Acts 16:14–15)

Or even the story of Rahab whose family were saved because of her faith:

> *"So the men said to her: 'We will be blameless of this oath of yours which you have made us swear, unless, when we come into the land, you bind this line of scarlet cord in the window through which you let us down, and unless you bring your father, your mother, your brothers, and all your father's household to your own home. So it shall be that whoever goes outside the doors of your house into the street, his blood shall be on his own head, and we will be guiltless. And whoever is with you in the house, his blood shall be on our head if a hand is laid on him.'"*
> (Joshua 2:17–19)

With such examples we can be sure that God is looking for someone in the family line who is committed, faithful and obedient to Him, whatever their status in the world's eyes.

The following is the story of two families as quoted in Tim and Bev LaHaye's book *Spirit Controlled Family*.[3] The first family was descended from Max Jukes from New York State who did not believe in Christian training. He was married to a girl of like mind. One thousand and twenty-six descendants were studied. It was found that three hundred descendants had died prematurely. One hundred were in jail for an average of thirteen years each. One hundred and ninety of their descendants became prostitutes. One hundred became drunkards. All together they cost the state of New York six million dollars. This was in 1978. They made no positive contribution to society.

The second family is that of a man called Jonathan Edwards who was from same state of New York. He also married a girl of like mind but this time they both believed in Christian training. Of seven hundred and twenty-nine descendants studied they found that there were three hundred preachers of the Gospel. There were sixty-five college professors and thirteen university presidents. Sixty of Jonathan's descendants were authors of good books. Three actually became USA Congressmen and one became a Vice-President of the United States of America. There is no record of Jonathan Edwards' family having cost the state anything. Rather, they made a strong positive contribution to society.

Does God want to bless you and your family? The answer from the Scriptures would definitely appear to be yes, if we put our faith in the Lord Jesus Christ and seek to obey God's commandments. Sometimes a "family tree" helps us to see what blessings God has, and is, causing to flow down our family line – you might like to copy and use the diagram in Figure 2 opposite.

Notes _____

1. D.M. Lloyd-Jones, *God's Ultimate Purpose*, Banner of Truth Trust, 1978.
2. Francis Frangipane, *The Power of Covenant Prayer*, Charisma House, America, 1998.
3. Tim and Bev Lahaye, *Spirit Controlled Family*, Kingsway Publications, 1978.

GREAT GRANDPARENTS

Paternal	*Maternal*
Grandfather & Grandmother	Grandfather & Grandmother
Grandfather & Grandmother	Grandfather & Grandmother

GRANDPARENTS

Grandfather Grandmother   Grandfather Grandmother

PARENTS

Father   Mother

SELF   **SIBLING**

Figure 2: **Generational Blessing**

Chapter 5

Hindrances to God's Blessing

We have already noted some of the requirements that need to be fulfilled in order for God's blessing to pass down the generational line. The importance of sowing good qualities into the family line, the importance of having faith in our Heavenly Father who works all things together for our good, as well as the importance of having a heart of obedience towards His commandments, are a great foundation. We can see also the reverse, that disobedience and unbelief are key hindrances to receiving blessing, because God has stressed that the opposite is so necessary. We are told in the Scriptures that:

> *"without faith it is impossible to please Him, for he who comes to God must believe that He is, and that He is a rewarder of those who diligently seek Him."*   (Hebrews 11:6)

Unbelief seems to hinder God's work in every area of our lives, for He is looking for those who will trust Him even through dark and difficult times. Such people choose to believe that God is at work behind the scenes even though they cannot see the outcome, and that He will indeed work all things together for good.

An instance of this would be the family of King Hezekiah: it would seem that this man's godly heritage was at risk of faltering because of his son Manasseh:

"Manasseh was twelve years old when he became king, and he reigned fifty-five years in Jerusalem. But he did evil in the sight of the LORD, according to the abominations of the nations whom the LORD had cast out before the children of Israel. For he rebuilt the high places which Hezekiah his father had broken down; he raised up altars for the Baals, and made wooden images; and he worshipped all the host of heaven and served them. He also built altars in the house of the LORD, of which the LORD had said, 'In Jerusalem shall My name be forever.' And he built altars for all the host of heaven in the two courts of the house of the LORD. Also he caused his sons to pass through the fire in the Valley of the Son of Hinnom; he practised soothsaying, used witchcraft and sorcery, and consulted mediums and spiritists. He did much evil in the sight of the LORD, to provoke Him to anger. He even set a carved image, the idol which he had made, in the house of God, of which God had said to David and to Solomon his son, 'In this house and in Jerusalem, which I have chosen out of all the tribes of Israel, I will put My name forever; and I will not again remove the foot of Israel from the land which I have appointed for your fathers – only if they are careful to do all that I have commanded them, according to the whole law and the statutes and the ordinances by the hand of Moses.' So Manasseh seduced Judah and the inhabitants of Jerusalem to do more evil than the nations whom the LORD had destroyed before the children of Israel. And the LORD spoke to Manasseh and his people, but they would not listen." (2 Chronicles 33:1–10)

What a dreadful scenario – surely God will wipe out Hezekiah's family line; the blessing must stop with Hezekiah. However, we go on to read that Manasseh repented and God did, in His mercy, restore him:

"Now when he was in affliction, he implored the LORD his God, and humbled himself greatly before the God of his fathers, and prayed to

Him; and He received his entreaty, heard his supplication, and brought him back to Jerusalem into his kingdom. Then Manasseh knew that the LORD was God." (2 Chronicles 33:12–13)

So whilst we may become disillusioned concerning our family line and begin to move in unbelief when we fail to see God's hand of blessing upon our present generation, we need to remember that our future descendants may be the ones to reap the consequences of our faithfulness and obedience.

We should not allow unbelief to hinder us, or our future descendants, from receiving what God desires to give to us. If one generation turns away from God's ways that in itself is not sufficient to make a judgment against generational blessing as a whole. However, we need to be aware that when an attitude of unbelief takes root it has the potential of hindering the flow of God's blessing and somewhere in the generational line there will need to be repentance and forgiveness.

There are a number of other hindrances to receiving the blessing of God: for example, that of disdaining God's blessing; dishonouring of God; ignoring our pledge to others; not caring for widows and orphans and robbing God of His dues.

Disdaining God's Blessing

An example of the latter is one of the most difficult stories in the Scriptures as regards an obstacle to God blessing His people: the story of Esau and Jacob. According to Malachi 1:2–3 we read that God says that He loved Jacob and hated Esau:

"Yet Jacob I have loved;
But Esau I have hated." (Malachi 1:2–3)

116

It is difficult to relate this scripture to the view that God's desire is to bless all of His children. According to R.T. Kendall the use of *love* and *hate* is a common Hebraic idiom which is not meant to be taken literally but is given as a comparison. Thus the meaning would be simply that Jacob "was preferred" over Esau. However, this doesn't alter the fact that God chooses some people to pour His blessing upon more than others. There is something here about the sovereignty of God.

When we compare this scripture with Hebrews 12:15–17 we can maybe glimpse some understanding of God's reasoning:

> *"looking carefully lest anyone fall short of the grace of God; lest any root of bitterness springing up cause trouble, and by this many become defiled; lest there be any fornicator or profane person like Esau, who for one morsel of food sold his birthright. For you know that afterward, when he wanted to inherit the blessing, he was rejected, for he found no place for repentance, though he sought it diligently with tears."*

Esau had voluntarily chosen to give up his birthright and live for present gratification, thus forfeiting God's special favour. It is quite interesting to note that Martin Luther said that he expected to see Esau in heaven, i.e. that the fact that God preferred Jacob did not mean that Esau was not loved but rather that God had a special love for Israel.

Dishonouring God

Dishonouring God is another way of hindering God's blessings. This is described in Malachi 2:1–2:

> *"'And now, O priests, this commandment is for you.*
> *If you will not hear,*

And if you will not take it to heart,
To give glory to My name,'
Says the LORD of hosts,
'I will send a curse upon you,
And I will curse your blessings.
Yes, I have cursed them already,
Because you do not take it to heart.
Behold, I will rebuke your descendants.'"

God is only able to bless those people who honour His name. Most of us will have seen the film *Chariots of Fire* which tells the story of one man who chose to forego fame, if necessary, in order to honour the Lord and the Sabbath day.

Conversely, we have the story of Eli the Priest who honoured his sons before God and suffered the consequences:

> *"Therefore the LORD God of Israel says: 'I said indeed that your house and the house of your father would walk before Me forever.' But now the LORD says: 'Far be it from Me; for those who honour Me I will honour, and those who despise Me shall be lightly esteemed.'"*

(1 Samuel 2:30)

The Scriptures affirm that if we do not honour God then a curse will replace the blessing:

> *"'And now, O priests, this commandment is for you.*
> *If you will not hear,*
> *And if you will not take it to heart,*
> *To give glory to My name,'*
> *Says the LORD of hosts,*
> *'I will send a curse upon you,*

> *And I will curse your blessings.*
> *Yes, I have cursed them already,*
> *Because you do not take it to heart.' "* (Malachi 2:1–2)

It is interesting that these words are addressed to a person who has been placed in a position of authority, a priest, and therefore whose words, as we will see in a moment, have the potential of having a deep influence over the congregation.

Ignoring Our Pledge to Others

An example of this would be the covenant which Joshua made with the Gibeonites that the Israelites would always protect them:

> *"So Joshua made peace with them, and made a covenant with them*
> *to let them live; and the rulers of the congregation swore to them."*
> (Joshua 9:15)

The fact that they were trapped into this covenant by the Gibeonites made no difference to the Lord when Saul in later years broke the covenant. God brought a famine upon the land – a curse instead of a blessing:

> *"Now there was a famine in the days of David for three years, year*
> *after year; and David inquired of the LORD. And the LORD answered,*
> *'It is because of Saul and his bloodthirsty house, because he killed the*
> *Gibeonites.' "* (2 Samuel 21:1)

This shows how seriously God takes a covenant which is made either between God and His people or between each other.

119

Not Caring for Widows and Orphans

Another blockage to staying in God's blessing would seem to be if we neglect to care for the poor, the widows and the orphans. As the prophet Isaiah writes:

> *"'Learn to do good;*
> *Seek justice,*
> *Rebuke the oppressor;*
> *Defend the fatherless,*
> *Plead for the widow.*
> *Come now, and let us reason together,'*
> *Says the LORD,*
> *'Though your sins are like scarlet,*
> *They shall be as white as snow;*
> *Though they are red like crimson,*
> *They shall be as wool.*
> *If you are willing and obedient,*
> *You shall eat the good of the land;*
> *But if you refuse and rebel,*
> *You shall be devoured by the sword';*
> *For the mouth of the LORD has spoken."* (Isaiah 1:17–20)

Robbing God of His Dues

Finally the Scriptures teach us that paying tithes is a requisite of living under God's blessing.

> *"'Will a man rob God?*
> *Yet you have robbed Me!*
> *But you say,*
> *"In what way have we robbed You?"*

In tithes and offerings.
You are cursed with a curse,
For you have robbed Me,
Even this whole nation.
Bring all the tithes into the storehouse,
That there may be food in My house,
And try Me now in this,'
Says the LORD *of hosts,*
'If I will not open for you the windows of heaven
And pour out for you such blessing
That there will not be room enough to receive it.
And I will rebuke the devourer for your sakes,
So that he will not destroy the fruit of your ground,
Nor shall the vine fail to bear fruit for you in the field,'
Says the LORD *of hosts."*　　　　　　　　　(Malachi 3:8–11)

Some people argue that tithing is an Old Testament principle and that Christians are under a new covenant and therefore do not need to give a tenth of their income to the Lord. There appear to be reasonable arguments on both sides of the debate, although as Christians it would seem to be apposite that all that we are and have belongs to the Lord and therefore at least a tenth would be given to church or charities. We have already seen that one of the laws of blessing is the law of sowing and reaping. I believe that this law is linked into the question of tithing.

According to the New Testament, if we sow sparingly then we will certainly reap sparingly, and conversely if we sow generously then we will certainly reap generously.

"But this I say: He who sows sparingly will also reap sparingly, and
he who sows bountifully will also reap bountifully. So let each one give

as he purposes in his heart, not grudgingly or of necessity; for God loves a cheerful giver. And God is able to make all grace abound toward you, that you, always having all sufficiency in all things, may have abundance for every good work." (2 Corinthians 9:6–8)

We are also reminded in the Scriptures that we cannot outgive God:

"Give, and it will be given to you: good measure, pressed down, shaken together, and running over will be put into your bosom. For with the same measure that you use, it will be measured back to you."

(Luke 6:38)

Chapter 6
Made in the Image of God

We have seen that it is the intention of God's heart to bless His creation, His people and their present-day families as well as their future generational lines. I firmly believe that it is also the intention of God's heart that we, His children, bless other people. This may be by our presence (being salt and light in the world) as well as by our actions towards other people. Another way in which we do this is through our words.

According to the book of Proverbs there is a great deal of power in the words which we speak. These can be either for good or ill. The writer of Proverbs states:

> *"Death and life are in the power of the tongue."*   (Proverbs 18:21)

From this scripture we can see that we can either bless others by speaking life into them or conversely curse them by speaking death into their spirits. Why is this so? I believe that there are two main reasons – the place of authority and the source from which they proceed.

Authority to Bless

The first and most important one is that of the position of authority which lies behind the one speaking the words. The

Scriptures affirm that it is out of the heart that the mouth speaks and if the person who is speaking is in a position of authority over us, then their words will carry great power. For example, parents hold a tremendous place of authority in a child's life and therefore the words which they speak have the potential of making a deep and lasting impression upon the child, either for good or ill. The power of the word lies in the authority which lies behind the word. This is true either of blessing or of curse: authority is the key.

God-given Delegated Authority

In the Scriptures men and women of faith knew the importance of being placed in a position of authority in order that they might speak out the truth which God had commanded them to declare. Take, for example, the faith which Abraham showed when he spoke words concerning his son Isaac:

> *"And Abraham said to his young men, 'Stay here with the donkey; the lad and I will go yonder and worship, **and we will come back to you.**'"*
> (Genesis 22:5, emphasis added)

Moses showed a similar faith when faced with the dilemma of the Red Sea:

> *"And Moses said to the people, 'Do not be afraid. **Stand still, and see the salvation of the Lord**, which He will accomplish for you today."*
> (Exodus 14:13, emphasis added)

Likewise when Joshua was faced with having to attack Jericho before the walls fell down he was given authority by the Lord to address the walls of Jericho:

*"And the L*ORD *said to Joshua: 'See! I have given Jericho into your hand.'"* (Joshua 6:2)

Also when David confronted Goliath he knew that his authority was centred upon the Lord:

*"This day the L*ORD *will deliver you into my hand, and I will strike you and take your head from you."* (1 Samuel 17:46)

And certainly Elijah was aware of his delegated authority when yet again he confronted Ahab:

*"As the L*ORD *God of Israel lives, before whom I stand, there shall not be dew nor rain these years, except at my word."*
(1 Kings 17:1)

Thus men of faith knew the necessity of speaking out what God had already spoken to them.

Delegated Authority by Society

As well as God delegating authority to certain people, so also does the society in which we live. For example, when a policeman stops you on the motorway for a motoring offence and commands you to pull over immediately, you promptly obey his words because he is in a position of authority, an authority delegated by society.

Teachers are also given authority by the community and as such are in an excellent position to speak words of blessing or cursing upon the children who are in their care. Truly they are *in locus parentis* (they have the delegated authority instead of a parent when they are teaching) and as such their words can be very powerful in the life of a child in much the same way as a parent's would be.

An article in the *Sunday Times*, on 25th July 2004, includes an extract from *The Boy with no Shoes* by the author William Horwood. This article gives a very apt description of the power of words to bless and encourage others. The well known children's writer tells how it was the words of a very special teacher who helped to drag him out of a sense of failure because of bullying and family rejection. William was terrified of examinations and especially became very frightened at the thought of taking the 11 plus examination after some very poor teaching.

On the night before the test his granny put some confidence into him through her words of encouragement. However, it was only after a new English master was put in charge of his class that he truly began to make remarkable progress. William writes about the way in which the new English master introduced himself:

> " 'This is the first lesson I have ever taught anyone,' he said, 'which means all of us, you and I, have . . . that we all have everything to gain.' It was the first positive thing any master had said to us.
>
> 'Now,' he said, 'I have been told that as a class you are "not very good at English" and might find O-levels "difficult". Let us deal with this misconception at once.' We stared. 'Do you realize that adults come from all over the world to England to learn English? And they find English very difficult. But I doubt that a single one of those adults would be able to speak English even half as well as each one of you already do. In short . . . each one of you is an expert at English language, so good in fact that people would pay each of you a great deal of money if you could teach them what you know.'

We sat thunderstruck.

'So I see no reason why in eight months' time you shouldn't pass your English language O-level.'

'But, sir?' It was Jowett. 'O-levels aren't, er, simple, are they?'

'Oh, but they are, Jowett, they are very simple. People like to make examinations seem difficult but really they are not. Now, repeat after me: "I am going to pass my O-level in English language next year."' We mumbled the words.

'Louder, please,' he said.

Soon we were roaring: 'I AM GOING TO PASS MY O-LEVEL ENGLISH LANGUAGE NEXT YEAR!'

The classroom door slammed open and Captain Flax stood there. 'What . . . ' he began, ' . . . is going on?' Mr Wharton's eyes grew steely behind his spectacles.

'I am very sorry if we have disturbed you, Captain Flax. Youthful enthusiasm . . . '

Then he did the unthinkable: he turned back to us and somehow consigned Captain Flax to the shadows. The door closed. Mr Wharton glanced towards it with the briefest of looks of intense dislike.

'Before this lesson ends,' he told us, 'I want to make something clear. There is an expectation that the pass rate in this class will not be high. But I do not like failure, because generally it is completely unnecessary.

'More importantly, I like the feeling of success. It breeds more success. I have very little interest in how this class may perform in other subjects, but in my subjects this form will do better than the Upper Fifth, better . . . '

Looking at our astonished faces, he said: 'But I see you do not believe that as a form you will do as well as the Upper Fifth. But you will succeed. One by one you will succeed just as, a long time ago, I began to succeed after a long time of not doing so.'"

What a wonderful description of the power of someone in a position of authority, using their ability to speak words of encouragement and blessing in order that a child could move from a position of failure to a place of success.

God's Inherent Authority

God, of course, has absolute inherent authority and we can see evidence of this through His spoken word at creation. We are told in the Scriptures that in the beginning God created the world through His Word – the uncreated Creator created out of His spirit through His Word:

> *"By faith we understand that the worlds were framed by the word of God, so that the things which are seen were not made of things which are visible."* (Hebrews 11:3)

God's Word in creation was so powerful and effective because it was backed by His inherent authority. God spoke and it was so. In the first chapter of the book of Genesis we repeatedly have the words *'And God said . . . and it was so.'* Therefore, we know that the spoken Word (not the deed) is the creating power: the Word comes before the deed: the Word produces the deed because it is supported by God's authority.

We note that God spoke in authority eight times during the creation of the world and each word produced a corresponding new state in the world. Throughout the first chapter of Genesis we see these words repeated time and again:

> *"Then God said . . . "*
> (Genesis 1:3; 1:6; 1:9; 1:11; 1:14; 1:20; 1:24; 1:26)

Notice that God spoke a blessing upon that which His Word had produced, i.e. the world. The blessing came when God pronounced *"it was very good"*.

> *"God saw everything that He had made, and indeed it was very good."*
> (Genesis 1:31)

God-given "Inherent Authority"

As well as society delegating authority to certain people within a community, we find that there are also positions of inherent authority given to certain roles within society. For example, the Prime Minister would have an authority which is inherent to his position as would, of course, the Queen.

In the same manner God Himself has given to certain people an inherent authority. This is an authority which is given and recognised by God: an authority which comes with the role. Parental authority would come into this category. Such an inherent authority has a tremendous potential for blessing, especially as far as words are concerned.

Parental Authority

Scripture gives us many such instances of fathers and mothers speaking words of blessing into their children's lives. We see this inherent parental authority and blessing through the actions of the father and mother of Rebekah (Laban and Bethuel) who spoke out their blessing on Rebekah on her forthcoming marriage to Isaac:

> *"So they sent away Rebekah their sister and her nurse, and Abraham's servant and his men. And they blessed Rebekah and **said to her**:*

> *'Our sister, may you become*
> *The mother of thousands of ten thousands;*
> *And may your descendants possess*
> *The gates of those who hate them.'"*
>
> (Genesis 24:59–60, emphasis added)

Likewise Laban, the father of Rachel and Leah, arose very early in the morning in order to bless his daughters before they left his home to travel away with Jacob:

> *"And early in the morning Laban arose, and kissed his sons and daughters and blessed them. Then Laban departed and returned to his place."* (Genesis 31:55)

A Father-in-Law's Blessing

The Scriptures also encourage us to believe that a father-in-law has an inherent authority to bless his son or daughter-in-law:

> *"So Moses went and returned to Jethro his father-in-law, and said to him, 'Please let me go and return to my brethren who are in Egypt, and see whether they are still alive.' And Jethro said to Moses, 'Go in peace.'"* (Exodus 4:18)

A Husband's Blessing

We know of course that God has given an inherent authority to husbands to speak words of blessing upon their wives:

> *"Her children rise up and call her blessed;*
> *Her husband also, and he praises her."* (Proverbs 31:28)

It is an interesting fact that the Scriptures seem to lay great store upon the power and influence of a husband's prayers for his wife. We see an example of this in Isaac's desperate prayers for Rebekah who couldn't conceive:

> *"Now Isaac pleaded with the LORD for his wife, because she was barren; and the LORD granted his plea, and Rebekah his wife conceived."*
>
> (Genesis 25:21)

A Grandfather's Blessing

Grandparents, and especially grandfathers, also have an inherent authority before the Lord in order that they might bless their grandchildren. Jacob was encouraged to do this by his son Joseph:

> *"And Joseph said to his father, 'They are my sons, whom God has given me in this place.' And he said, 'Please bring them to me, and I will bless them.'"*
>
> (Genesis 48:9)

When Joseph brought his sons to his father, Jacob, in order that he might indeed bless them, Jacob spoke out a wonderful grandfatherly blessing:

> *"God, before whom my fathers Abraham and Isaac walked,*
> *The God who has fed me all my life long to this day,*
> *The Angel who has redeemed me from all evil,*
> *Bless the lads;*
> *Let my name be named upon them,*
> *And the name of my fathers Abraham and Isaac;*
> *And let them grow into a multitude in the midst of the earth."*
>
> (Genesis 48:15–16)

I love the phrase *"Bless the lads"* because it sounds very much like the idiom of my grandfather who was from Wearside in County Durham and would have said something very similar concerning his grandchildren!

Jacob continued with his blessing, putting the youngest grandson before the eldest:

> *"So he blessed them that day, saying, 'By you Israel will bless, saying, "May God make you as Ephraim and as Manasseh!"' And thus he set Ephraim before Manasseh."*　　　　　　　　(Genesis 48:20)

The words of a grandparent can be very powerful either for good or ill. Speaking from personal experience, I remember many of the words which my grandfather pronounced over me which have truly been a foundation of blessing throughout my life.

A Leader's Blessing

According to the Scriptures leaders are in a prime position to speak words of blessing into people's lives. For example, in the Scriptures we see that the priest is in a special position of leadership and as such his words have the power to bless.

A Priest's Blessing

The priests were God's representatives and they had inherent authority to speak a blessing of peace upon the congregation:

> *"Speak to Aaron and his sons, saying, 'This is the way you shall bless the children of Israel. Say to them:*

> *"The LORD bless you and keep you;*
> *The LORD make His face shine upon you,*
> *And be gracious to you;*
> *The LORD lift up His countenance upon you,*
> *And give you peace."'"* (Numbers 6:23–26)

And so Aaron, as a priest, blessed the people:

> *"Then Aaron lifted his hand toward the people, blessed them ..."*
> (Leviticus 9:22)

When Hannah was distraught because she couldn't have children, Eli the priest spoke words of blessing over her:

> *"Then Eli answered and said, 'Go in peace, and the God of Israel grant your petition which you have asked of Him.'"* (1 Samuel 1:17)

These words had the power to lift Hannah from a place of deep sorrow and suffering into one of hope and expectancy.

John Kilpatrick, pastor of Brownsville Assembly of God Church in Pensacola, Florida, lists "priestly blessing" as one of the keys to the revival which broke out in his church on the 18th of June 1995.[1]

A King's Blessing

Under God we see that kings are also in a position of authority and thus King David blesses the people and his household:

> *"And when David had finished offering burnt offerings and peace offerings, he blessed the people in the name of the LORD of hosts."*
> (2 Samuel 6:18)

David, of course, also had the authority to bless his household as a husband:

> "*Then David returned to bless his household. And Michal the daughter of Saul came out to meet David . . .* " (2 Samuel 6:20)

King Solomon blessed the people:

> "*Then the king turned around and blessed the whole assembly of Israel, while all the assembly of Israel was standing.*" (1 Kings 8:14)

The Blessing of Jesus

Jesus is the prime example of one who moved in great authority and blessed people through His words:

> "*Then they were all amazed and spoke among themselves, saying, 'What a word this is! For with authority and power He commands the unclean spirits, and they come out.'* " (Luke 4:36)

Jesus based His authority on the fact that He was a Son of the Father – His was both inherent as well as delegated authority:

> "*While he was still speaking, behold, a bright cloud overshadowed them; and suddenly a voice came out of the cloud, saying, 'This is My beloved Son, in whom I am well pleased. Hear Him!'* " (Matthew 17:5)

As a Son He had an inherent authority but He was also aware that He only had authorization to do what He saw the Father doing (delegated authority):

"Then Jesus said to them . . . 'I do nothing of Myself; but as My Father taught Me, I speak these things.'" (John 8:28)

Jesus is also described as a great High Priest and as such He has the authority to bless His followers:

"And He led them out as far as Bethany, and He lifted up His hands and blessed them." (Luke 24:50)

He also is a King with great and total authority. The wonderful truth is that He has delegated authority to those who follow Him:

"And Jesus came and spoke to them, saying, 'All authority has been given to Me in heaven and on earth. Go therefore and make disciples of all the nations, baptizing them in the name of the Father and of the Son and of the Holy Spirit, teaching them to observe all things that I have commanded you; and lo, I am with you always, even to the end of the age.' Amen." (Matthew 28:18–20)

"Behold, I give you the authority to trample on serpents and scorpions, and over all the power of the enemy, and nothing shall by any means hurt you." (Luke 10:19)

The authority which we have been given through Jesus manifests itself in a number of ways. For instance we are:

Created Creators

We have been made in the image of God and thus we are **created creators**. How do we create? We create out of our spirit by speaking things into being according to God's Word. In the

Scriptures there is an immense emphasis upon the spoken word. Why is this? It would seem to be that speaking out God's truth is a spiritual act of taking and using by faith that which God has promised will be, with the proviso that God has spoken the *rhema* Word to us in the first place as an individual and not just a collective word for everyone. As it says in the Scriptures:

> " . . . *man shall not live by bread alone; but man lives by every word that proceeds from the mouth of the* LORD.*"*   (Deuteronomy 8:3)

Before we can speak God's Word with authority we need to hear the Word of God spoken to us by the Holy Spirit. As Steve Sampson says in his book *You Can Hear the Voice of God*,[2] "You must hear the Holy Spirit (the author of Scripture) in your particular situation."

Not only do we need to hear the Holy Spirit but we also need to speak out what He says in order for blessings to follow.

Children of God

We have also been given authority as **children of God**:

> *"But as many as received Him, to them He gave the right to become children of God, to those who believe in His name: who were born, not of blood, nor of the will of the flesh, nor of the will of man, but of God."*   (John 1:12–13)

As God's children we have been given the right to speak in His name, with the proviso that, like Jesus, we only speak what the Father gives us to speak, which means, of course, that we need to spend much time in His presence in order to listen to His heart.

As His children we have also been given authority to bless others by commanding demons to depart and diseases to be healed:

> *"Then He called His twelve disciples together and gave them power and authority over all demons, and to cure diseases."* (Luke 9:1)

Priests and Kings

We are also described in the Scriptures as both **priests and kings** and as such we have the inherent authority that comes with these roles. We are told in the book of Revelation that Jesus:

> *"has made us kings and priests to His God and Father, to Him be glory and dominion forever and ever. Amen."* (Revelation 1:6)

As such we are able to bless others with our words of *shalom*. According to the *Wycliffe Bible Commentary* the word *shalom* is a much more comprehensive word than "peace". It also includes the concepts of completeness, security, health, tranquillity, contentment, friendship, and peace with God and man. What a privilege we have been given as priests to speak such words of blessing to the people whom we meet.

> *"But you are a chosen generation, a royal priesthood."*
>
> (1 Peter 2:9)

Blessing God

We are also encouraged to:

> *"Bless God in the congregations."* (Psalm 68:26)

There are many references in the Scriptures as to how our words have the potential of blessing God:

> *"And He led them out as far as Bethany, and He lifted up His hands and blessed them. Now it came to pass, while He blessed them, that He was parted from them and carried up into heaven. And they worshipped Him, and returned to Jerusalem with great joy, and were continually in the temple praising and blessing God."*   (Luke 24:50–53)

Blessing our Enemies

With our words we are even commanded to bless our enemies:

> *"But I say to you, love your enemies, bless those who curse you, do good to those who hate you, and pray for those who spitefully use you and persecute you."*   (Matthew 5:44)

> *"Bless those who persecute you; bless and do not curse."*
>
> (Romans 12:14)

Blessing the Jewish Nation

We are encouraged to bless the Jewish people and we are told that that will bring a blessing upon ourselves:

> *"I will make you a great nation;*
> *I will bless you*
> *And make your name great;*
> *And you shall be a blessing.*
> *I will bless those who bless you,*
> *And I will curse him who curses you;*
> *And in you all the families of the earth shall be blessed."*
>
> (Genesis 12:2–3)

Blessing the Sick

We are also confident that our words can bless those who are sick, for our words will have the potential of bringing them into a state of health:

> *"Pleasant words are like a honeycomb,*
> *Sweetness to the soul and health to the bones."*   (Proverbs 16:24)

A very good friend of ours, a Methodist Minister, developed very bad pains in his chest. His doctor did some tests and eventually diagnosed angina. Our friend was not convinced that it was angina and so he eventually went to stay at a Healing Centre at Crowhurst. The man in charge of the ministry there was chatting to him one day and asked him: "Who stabbed you in the chest?" Our friend remembered that a number of months prior to feeling the pain, a church steward had poked him in the chest about some church matter, saying angrily: "You'll suffer for this." The man in charge at Crowhurst prayed for him – he figuratively removed the arrows from his chest and prayed healing and the blessing of health into him. Our friend can now run up hills and go for long walks without getting out of breath and he has had no more pain. Thus we have a clear example of a person in leadership (a church steward) who used his words in a wrong manner to bring disease upon someone and another person in leadership who used his words to bless him. Thus our words have the potential to be a blessing or a curse.

Notes
1. John Kilpatrick, *Feast of Fire*, Marshall Pickering, 1995.
2. Steve Sampson, *You Can Hear the Voice of God*, Sovereign World, 2003.

Chapter 7

Source from which Words Proceed

The second reason why our words are so powerful and effective is because of the source from which they proceed. From where do our words originate? Do our words simply come from our mouth? Do they come from our soul area – our minds, our emotions or our will? Or do they come from the very centre of our being – from our heart – from our innermost being?

I believe that words emanate from the very heart of a person and therefore the power of the word lies in the fact that they are touched by the state of the heart of the other person. If the words come from a critical hard heart they will have the potential of bringing a curse; if they come from a gentle loving heart they will have the potential of bringing a blessing. Therefore the words which are spoken by another person can touch my inner being for either good or ill.

Thus we see that our words have the potential of bringing forth much blessing and fruitfulness into the lives of other people. The River of Life in the Scriptures is very often a picture of the work of the Holy Spirit. For our words to bless others our words need to flow from the Holy Spirit and then they will be life-giving and a blessing to other people.

In the Scriptures Jesus is described as the Word of God:

"In the beginning was the Word, and the Word was with God, and the Word was God. He was in the beginning with God. All things were made through Him, and without Him nothing was made that was made." (John 1:1–3)

And truly through His words much healing ensued: Jesus knew the power of words; He often spoke to the condition with which He was faced. Sometimes His Word was a word of rebuke. For example, He rebuked a fever:

"So He stood over her and rebuked the fever, and it left her."
(Luke 4:39)

He also rebuked a demon and the person was delivered:

"But Jesus rebuked him, saying, 'Be quiet, and come out of him!'"
(Mark 1:25)

Sometimes He spoke a Word of healing, as He did to a leper:

"Then Jesus put out His hand and touched him, saying, 'I am willing; be cleansed.' Immediately his leprosy was cleansed."
(Matthew 8:3)

And also to the centurion:

"And Jesus said to him, 'I will come and heal him.' The centurion answered and said, 'Lord, I am not worthy that You should come under my roof. But only speak a word, and my servant will be healed.'"
(Matthew 8:7–8)

He spoke a word of healing to some blind men:

> *"And when He had come into the house, the blind men came to Him. And Jesus said to them, 'Do you believe that I am able to do this?' They said to Him, 'Yes, Lord.' Then He touched their eyes, saying, 'According to your faith let it be to you.' And their eyes were opened."*
>
> (Matthew 9:28–30)

We need to learn how to direct our words into a person's inner being – to speak life, healing, freedom and blessing into them.

Conversely, of course, our words can become a curse rather than a blessing. According to Proverbs 18:21:

> *"Death and life are in the power of the tongue."*

So we see that it is possible to speak either words of life and blessing into another's life or speak death and a curse.

Until a certain age parents are as God to a child and if our parents have made pronouncements over us in the past, such as, "You're useless, hopeless, you're no good, you're pathetic, and nobody will ever want to marry you," we believe them and the words have the potential of going straight into our spirit. We begin to live according to their expectation of us.

Likewise the pronouncements of a husband or wife can also go very deep, for example, if there is verbal abuse by one spouse to the other using such words as: "You are pathetic," "You're a slob," "You're not a man, you're a mouse."

We have already noted the important place of authority that a grandparent has in a child's life. One woman who could never understand why she lived her life cloaked in deep shame was very interested to be told by her mother that she was illegitimate and that her grandfather had spoken words of shame over her whilst she was in the womb: "This child is a disgrace to this family – get out of my sight, I don't want to see it." One can understand why she lived her life cloaked in shame.

A baby can perceive in its young spirit much more than we maybe realise. So, if a baby hears such words as: "I hate this baby; he will never amount to anything," that pronouncement can have a long and lasting effect upon its young life.

However, the words of any authority figures can have a lasting and devastating effect. A lady, who I will call Elsie, was shattered when her first baby died of cot death when it was only four months old. She went to bed every evening, very distressed, telling her husband that she didn't want to wake up the next morning. One night the Lord came to her, wrapped her in a blanket of love, and she woke her husband to tell him it was all right although she still suffered great pain and grief.

Her grief had been deepened by her doctor saying to her one day, regarding her baby's death: "That's the worst of you modern mothers. You won't pick up your babies if they cry." That was not true of her, but she said that for twenty-one years she couldn't pass a crying baby without a great and an overwhelming longing to pick it up and feeling guilty for not doing so. It is interesting that by that time her baby would have been an adult!

The novelist Fay Weldon writes of when her husband was referred to a therapist after a minor heart attack. The therapist decided that Fay was the problem and that she and her husband were incompatible. The headline stated: "A therapist told her husband that their passion was a lie, and heartbreak and divorce followed."[1]

Inner Vows

It would appear, therefore, that our words have the ability to either bless or to curse other people or even ourselves. Inner vows are words, which we speak against ourselves very often as young children, and since they often come out of a wounded heart they bind themselves to us for the rest of our lives until God sets us free. For example: "I'm no good," "I'll never marry," "I'll never cry again," "I'll never trust a woman again," "No woman is ever going to tell me what to do," "I look awful," "I'll never make old bones!"

A woman who, as a little girl, saw her mother go into spontaneous labour vowed, "I'm never going to have children." And she never did!

The Power of God's Word

God's Word is a very powerful tool in the healing ministry. In fact, it is so powerful that it is able to divide between spirit and soul, thus enabling God to touch other people in their human spirits, through us, as we speak the Word of God into their lives. The Scriptures are described as the "sword of the Holy Spirit":

> " . . . *the sword of the Spirit, which is the word of God.*"
>
> (Ephesians 6:17)

> "*For the word of God is living and powerful, and sharper than any two-edged sword, piercing even to the division of soul and spirit, and of joints and marrow, and is a discerner of the thoughts and intents of the heart.*"
>
> (Hebrews 4:12)

Healing

We are told that God's Word brings healing:

> "*He sent His word and healed them.*"
>
> (Psalm 107:20)

Life-giving

God's Word is Life-giving:

> *"holding fast the word of life, so that I may rejoice in the day of Christ . . . "* (Philippians 2:16)

Jesus said:

> *"The words that I speak to you are spirit, and they are life."* (John 6:63)

Creative

God's Word is creative: it brings into being things which are not. We have already seen that God created the world through His Word – the uncreated Creator created out of His Spirit through His Word:

> *"By faith we understand that the worlds were framed by the word of God, so that the things which are seen were not made of things which are visible."* (Hebrews 11:3)

Therefore, we know that the spoken word (not the deed) is the creating power; the word comes before the deed; the word produces the deed.

The Place of Faith

Faith is the bridge between knowing your authority, knowing the will of the Father, and speaking it into being. Faith reaches out to God – receives the word from Him and speaks it into being. You cannot speak into existence what you have not received by faith, nor can you keep it within you because then it will not achieve what God intended.

Notes

1. *The Times* newspaper, times 2, 6th September, 2005, p. 4.

Chapter 8
Keys to Freedom

The Tree of Life

There is a very interesting reference in the Scriptures to the fact that our tongue is like a tree of life, and knowing how to use our tongues in a positive way is the route to freedom, both for ourselves and for other people for whom we may be called upon to pray.

> "A wholesome tongue is a tree of life."   (Proverbs 15:4)

According to the well known and respected commentator C.J. Ellicott, a wholesome tongue is "one which heals and soothes by its gentleness and judicious words".[1] It is interesting to trace the references to the tree of life throughout the Scriptures as to what its properties are and what effect it has upon a situation or person. The tree of life is, of course, mentioned in the first and the last books of the Bible. In Genesis chapter 2 we have the first reference to this tree, where we are told that:

> "The tree of life was also in the midst of the garden."
>
> (Genesis 2:9)

Whilst in the last book of the Bible we learn that:

> *"In the middle of its street, and on either side of the river, was the tree of life, which bore twelve fruits, each tree yielding its fruit every month. The leaves of the tree were for the healing of the nations."*
>
> (Revelation 22:2)

Matthew Henry, commentating upon this passage, writes:

> "As to this tree, observe,
>
> 1. The situation of it . . . This tree of life is fed by the pure waters of the river that comes from the throne of God.
> 2. The fruitfulness of this tree. (1) It brings forth many sorts of fruit – twelve sorts, suited to the refined taste of all the saints. (2) It brings forth fruit at all times – yields its fruit every month. This tree is never empty, never barren; there is always fruit upon it."[2]

What a wonderful thought that because our tongue is a tree of life it can speak life into the inward parts. This is especially true of speaking and affirming God's Word to our spirits.

> *"And you shall know the truth, and the truth shall make you free."*
>
> (John 8:32)

By taking hold of one of God's promises and affirming it to our inner man we will find the freedom that God's Word brings.

However, it is also true of our own words, for example by speaking such encouraging words as, "I can do it", "I like the way I did that", "I can do all things through Christ who strengthens me," we can move from a position of weakness to a position of strength. Positive words are powerful and life-enhancing.

On the other hand, we can also use our tongues against ourselves! Negative words can speak lies into our spirits: one man who said about himself, "I may as well be dead," had a stroke three days later and was dead within the month. Another person frequently said about himself, "I'm out of here," and in fact moved away from his good position of employment shortly afterwards. Our words are meant to encourage, affirm, build up, challenge and speak truth both into our lives and also into the lives of other people. Some of us will need to repent for the words we have used to poison, wound or damage ourselves or other people!

The Word of God

One of the most important keys to being freed from the effects of damaging and negative words is to allow Jesus Himself, who is the Word of God, to speak truth into the inner being of a person through the Holy Spirit. He can reach down into our innermost depths and supplant the darkness with the light of His truth, thus bringing His Kingdom into every part of us:

> *"The entrance of Your words gives light;*
> *It gives understanding to the simple."* (Psalm 119:130)

How does Jesus do that? He does it by opening our understanding to His truth through the Scriptures. It is important to remember that, even in the natural world, for our minds to understand something it takes another mind to explain it to us. Thus we rely on the mind of the Holy Spirit to inform our minds of the truth of the Scriptures which He has inspired as well as the truth of any painful situation which we may find ourselves in.

The Holy Spirit also brings revelation into our human spirits through His Word. The Holy Spirit takes the inspired Word from the Scriptures and plants it firmly into our human spirits thus displacing the lies, which we have believed, with His truth.

Jesus the Light of the World

Sometimes the Lord, as the Light of the World, will include another person in order to bring truth and light to the one in need. This would especially be true where the wounding from negative words has gone very deep. For example, the way in which I would proceed if I was ministering to someone would be as follows:

- After the person has shared the situation with me we would spend a little time waiting upon the Holy Spirit for His guidance.
- As we wait He may bring a memory to the surface that has a number of buried lies, negative words, curses and darkness within.
- I would ask Him to enter the "memory room" as the Light of the World and reveal the truth and the lies and negativity which are in that room.
- With the person's involvement and permission I will ask the Holy Spirit to challenge the lies and confront the darkness and begin to bring His truth to the fore.

When I was ministering in one church in Canada a lady came forward for ministry. She was absolutely heartbroken because her cat had died. As she shared her story with me I felt quite distinctly that she was suffering from a deeper grief than that for her beloved cat. She told me a little of her life story and then we decided to wait upon the Holy Spirit for more insight. As we waited she suddenly began to sob even more. After a while she shared the memory which the Holy Spirit was bringing to the surface. It was of a time when she was fifteen and quite permissive and rebellious. She had had a number of sexual partners and eventually went on to have an abortion. She had subsequently become a Christian. During the following year she convinced herself that she had never had an abortion, that she was unlovable and that the only one that could possibly love her was her cat. That is why the death of her cat was so devastating. As the Holy Spirit revealed the truth to her she acknowledged the truth about her baby and began to move into true grief. The Holy Spirit then revealed how much God loved and forgave her and wanted to restore her.

- I would break the power of any negative words or curses which the person has believed.
- The person will then need to work with the Holy Spirit in refuting the lies of the enemy as well as the human lies which he or she has swallowed and replace them with the truth of the Word of God.

"You shall know the truth, and the truth shall make you free."
(John 8:32)

– **Negative words**: "I'll never forgive myself."

God's Word says:

"'Come now, and let us reason together,'
Says the LORD,
'Though your sins are like scarlet,

> *They shall be as white as snow;*
> *Though they are red like crimson,*
> *They shall be as wool.'"*
>
> (Isaiah 1:18)

– **Negative words**: "I can't do anything."

God's Word says:

> *"I can do all things through Christ who strengthens me."*
>
> (Philippians 4:13)

– **Negative words**: "I'll never be free."

God's Word says:

> *"If the Son makes you free, you shall be free indeed."*
>
> (John 8:36)

– **Negative words**: "I am really frightened."

God's Word says:

> *"Fear not, for I have redeemed you;*
> *I have called you by your name;*
> *You are Mine."*
>
> (Isaiah 43:1)

– **Negative words**: "God cannot love me."

God's Word says:

> *"I have loved you with an everlasting love."*
>
> (Jeremiah 31:3)

– **Negative words**: "I am all alone."

God's Word says:

> *"He Himself has said, 'I will never leave you nor forsake you.'"*
>
> (Hebrews 13:5)

- **Negative words**: "I am not worth anything."

God's Word says:

> *"Since you were precious in My sight,*
> *You have been honoured,*
> *And I have loved you."* (Isaiah 43:4)

- **Negative words**: "It's impossible."

God's Word says:

> *"The things which are impossible with men are possible with*
> *God."* (Luke 18:27)

- Thus Jesus, who is the Truth, the Holy Spirit who is the Spirit of Truth, and the Word of God, which is the Word of Truth, will move the person into the place of wholeness.

Finally, we would do well to take note of God's way of blessing and speak it to ourselves and to others as the opportunity arises:

> *"And the LORD spoke to Moses, saying: 'Speak to Aaron and his sons,*
> *saying, "This is the way you shall bless the children of Israel. Say to them:*
>
> *'The LORD bless you and keep you;*
> *The LORD make His face shine upon you,*
> *And be gracious to you;*
> *The LORD lift up His countenance upon you,*
> *And give you peace.'"'"* (Numbers 6:22–26)

Questions to Consider

- What lies or half-truths have you swallowed? Ask the Holy Spirit for revelation.

- How do you use the sword of your spirit – your tongue?
    - Do you seek to encourage yourself?
    - Do you slander yourself?
    - Do you use threats against yourself?
    - Do you build yourself up or tear yourself down?
    - Do you build others up or pull them down?

- What hurtful words have you said recently?
  Seek forgiveness.
- What hurtful words have been said over you?
  Offer forgiveness.
- What positive words have you spoken so far today?
  Be encouraged.

Ask the Holy Spirit for a verse from Scripture to take with you into the coming week.

Notes _____

1. C.J. Ellicott, DD, (editor), *Bible Commentary, Volume 4*, Cassell and Co. Ltd.
2. Matthew Henry's *Commentary, Volume 10*, William Mackenzie, London.

Appendix:

Family Lines of Adam, Abraham and Rahab

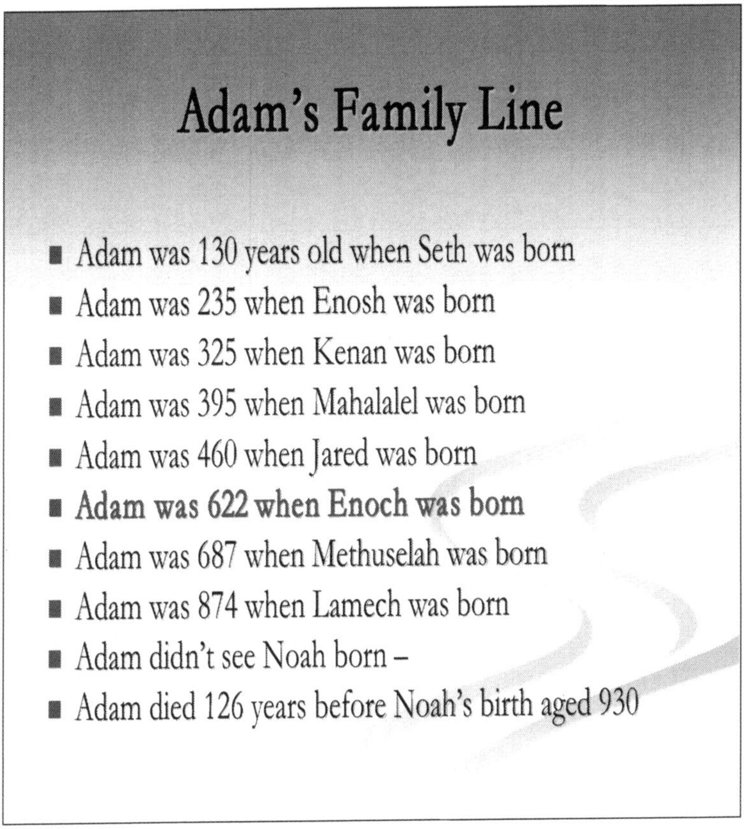

Adam's Family Line

- Adam was 130 years old when Seth was born
- Adam was 235 when Enosh was born
- Adam was 325 when Kenan was born
- Adam was 395 when Mahalalel was born
- Adam was 460 when Jared was born
- **Adam was 622 when Enoch was born**
- Adam was 687 when Methuselah was born
- Adam was 874 when Lamech was born
- Adam didn't see Noah born –
- Adam died 126 years before Noah's birth aged 930

Figure 3: Adam's Family Line

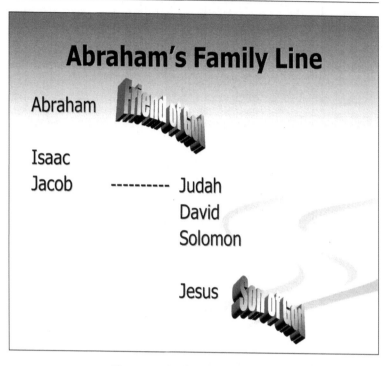

Figure 4: Abraham's Family Line

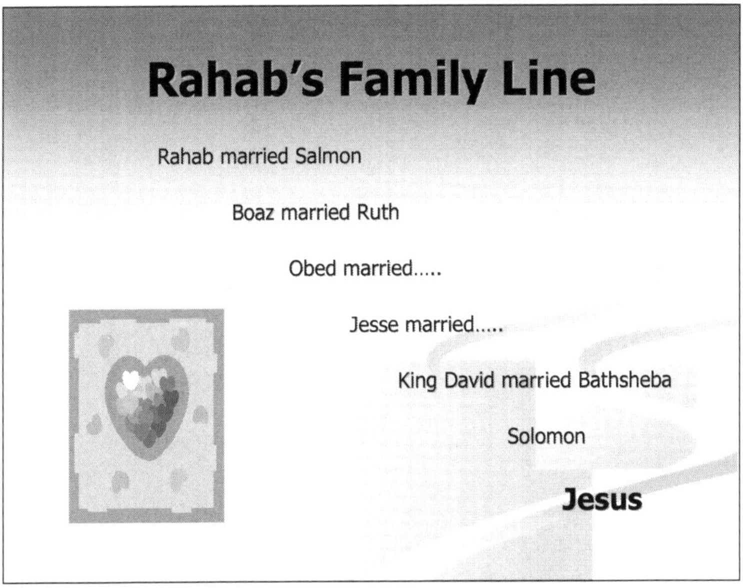

Rahab's Family Line

Rahab married Salmon

Boaz married Ruth

Obed married.....

Jesse married.....

King David married Bathsheba

Solomon

Jesus

Figure 5: **Rahab's Family Line**

We hope you enjoyed reading this New Wine book.
For details of other New Wine books
and a wide range of titles from other
Word and Spirit publishers visit our website:
www.newwineministries.co.uk
email: newwine@xalt.co.uk

*9 7 8 1 9 0 5 9 9 1 8 9 1 *

An environmentally friendly book printed and bound in England by www.printondemand-worldwide.com

PEFC Certified

This product is
from sustainably
managed forests
and controlled
sources

www.pefc.org

PEFC/16-33-415

®

MIX

Paper from
responsible sources

FSC® C004959

FSC

www.fsc.org

This book is made entirely of sustainable materials; FSC paper for the cover and PEFC paper for the text pages.

Reprint of # - C0 - 216/138/13 - PB - Lamination Matt - Printed on 16-Aug-17 13:06